effective
PRESENTING

chartered
management
institute

inspiring leaders

effective
PRESENTING

BRIAN SALTER

HODDER
EDUCATION
PART OF HACHETTE LIVRE UK

The publisher has used its best endeavours to ensure that the URLs for external websites referred to in this book are correct and active at the time of going to press. However, the publisher and the author have no responsibility for the websites and can make no guarantee that a site will remain live or that the content will remain relevant, decent or appropriate.

Orders: Please contact Bookpoint Ltd, 130 Milton Park, Abingdon, Oxon OX14 4SB. Telephone: (44) 01235 827720, Fax: (44) 01235 400454. Lines are open from 9.00 to 5.00, Monday to Saturday, with a 24-hour message answering service. You can also order through our website www.hoddereducation.co.uk.

British Library Cataloguing in Publication Data
A catalogue record for this title is available from the British Library.

ISBN: 978 0340 985 182

First published	2009
Impression number	10 9 8 7 6 5 4 3 2 1
Year	2012 2011 2010 2009

Copyright © 2009 Brian Salter

Cover image © Photodisk, Inc.

Photographer [logo] – Niki Sianni
The room layouts in Chapter 7 are reproduced with the kind permission of Amanda Vickers and Steve Bavister and are taken from *Teach Yourself Presenting* (Hodder 2007, ISBN 978 0340 941 751)

Typeset by Transet Limited, Coventry, England.
Printed in Great Britain for Hodder Education, part of Hachette UK, 338 Euston Road, London NW1 3BH by CPI Cox & Wyman Ltd, Reading, Berkshire, RG1 8EX.

Hachette UK's policy is to use papers that are natural, renewable and recyclable products and made from wood grown in sustainable forests. The logging and manufacturing processes are expected to conform to the environmental regulations of the country of origin.

The Chartered Management Institute

chartered
management
institute
inspiring leaders

The Chartered Management Institute is the only chartered professional body that is dedicated to management and leadership. We are committed to raising the performance of business by championing management.

We represent 71,000 individual managers and have 450 corporate members. Within the Institute there are also a number of distinct specialisms, including the Institute of Business Consulting and Women in Management Network.

We exist to help managers tackle the management challenges they face on a daily basis by raising the standard of management in the UK. We are here to help individuals become better managers and companies develop better managers.

We do this through a wide range of products and services, from practical management checklists to tailored training and qualifications. We produce research on the latest 'hot' management issues, provide a vast array of useful information through our online management information centre, as well as offering consultancy services and career information.

You can access these resources 'off the shelf' or we can provide solutions just for you. Our range of products and services is designed to ensure companies and managers develop their potential and excel. Whether you are at the start of your career or a proven performer in the boardroom, we have something for you.

We engage policy makers and opinion formers and, as the leading authority on management, we are regularly consulted on a range of management issues. Through our in-depth research and regular policy surveys of members, we have a deep understanding of the latest management trends.

For more information visit our website **www.managers.org.uk** or call us on **01536 207307**.

chartered
management
institute
inspiring leaders

Chartered Manager

Transform the way you work
The Chartered Management Institute's Chartered Manager award is the ultimate accolade for practising professional managers. Designed to transform the way you think about your work and how you add value to your organisation, it is based on demonstrating measurable impact.

This unique award proves your ability to make a real difference in the workplace.

Chartered Manager focuses on the six vital business skills of:

- Leading people
- Managing change
- Meeting customer needs
- Managing information and knowledge
- Managing activities and resources
- Managing yourself

Transform your organisation
There is a clear and well-established link between good management and improved organisational performance. Recognising this, the Chartered Manager scheme requires individuals to demonstrate how they are applying their leadership and change management skills to make significant impact within their organisation.

Transform your career
Whatever career stage a manager is at Chartered Manager will set them apart. Chartered Manager has proven to be a stimulus to career progression, either via recognition by their current employer or through the motivation to move on to more challenging roles with new employers.

But don't take just our word for it ...

Chartered Manager has transformed the careers and organisations of managers in all sectors.

- *'Being a Chartered Manager was one of the main contributing factors which led to my recent promotion.'*
  Lloyd Ross, Programme Delivery Manager, British Nuclear Fuels

- *'I am quite sure that a part of the reason for my success in achieving my appointment was due to my Chartered Manager award which provided excellent, independent evidence that I was a high quality manager.'*
  Donaree Marshall, Head of Programme Management Office, Water Service, Belfast

- *'The whole process has been very positive, giving me confidence in my strengths as a manager but also helping me to identify the areas of my skills that I want to develop. I am delighted and proud to have the accolade of Chartered Manager.'*
  Allen Hudson, School Support Services Manager, Dudley Metropolitan County Council

- *'As we are in a time of profound change, I believe that I have, as a result of my change management skills, been able to provide leadership to my staff. Indeed, I took over three teams and carefully built an integrated team, which is beginning to perform really well. I believe that the process I went through to gain Chartered Manager status assisted me in achieving this and consequently was of considerable benefit to my organisation.'*
  George Smart, SPO and D/Head of Resettlement, HM Prison Swaleside

To find out more or to request further information please visit our website **www.managers.org.uk/cmgr** or call us on **01536 207429**.

Contents

CHAPTER 03

CHAPTER 04

CHAPTER 05

HOW CAN I ADD FLAVOUR TO MY PRESENTATION TO MAKE IT MORE INTERESTING? 73

CHAPTER 06

HOW CAN I BEST PREPARE FOR THE PRESENTATION? 93

CHAPTER 07

CHAPTER 08

CHAPTER 09

CHAPTER 10

Preface

What do we mean by presentation? Why is it so important to be effective when we present? Why on earth do we need a book to tell us how to be effective in our presentations anyway?

Presentations occur in every aspect of life and can cover a whole gamut of different situations. For most of my working life – be it as a radio or TV broadcaster, directing public relations activities, staging events, being a company director, simply seeking financial backing for a great idea, or even training others in presentational techniques – I have been involved with presenting in one form or another and it never ceases to amaze me how so many people think they can get away with just opening their mouths and hoping that whatever they have to say will make an impact on others.

This isn't something that is unique or particular to one part of the world either. I have worked not only in the UK, but across Europe, the United States, and latterly in the Middle East. The problems and opportunities are the same. Of course, the customs change from country to country, but the underlying aspects of good presentational techniques remain constant.

To see the way some businesses are run, you'd think that the last thing they really want to do is to communicate with their customers. Customers, as we all know, are tyrants, and life would be so much easier without having to try to pander to their every whim! Unfortunately though, it is a fundamental fact of business that without customers there would be no revenues and therefore, by definition, no business.

But even outside the heady realms of big business, being able to present effectively is one of life's skills that can play a large part in our personal development, in our relationships with other people, and, of course, in how successful we are – however we decide to define that word 'success'.

To misquote the 'old bard':

Some people are born presenters; some are able to achieve presentational competence while others have presentations thrust upon them.

This book pulls together many of the techniques I have learned throughout my career, and is also a distillation of much that I teach on my training courses. I have used a number of examples taken from my days in broadcasting, not only in the BBC, but more recently within the Middle East.

Although, in the main, the protagonists remain anonymous within the pages of this book, I would, all the same, like to say a big thank you to them all for giving me inspiration over the years.

In particular, thanks must go to Veronica Manoukian, my mentor par-excellence from those heady BBC days in the 1970s; to John Tusa with whom I was privileged to work when he broadcast regularly on the BBC World Service before moving on to even greater heights; to my ex-colleagues in Saudi Arabian Television – especially Huda Zariwala, Cyma Aziz, Ghalya Al-Attar and Hassan Sheikh; to Anna-Denise Ioannou in Qatar, Zeena Zalamea in Dubai and Miam Medrano in Hong Kong; and to all my family, friends and other work colleagues who, despite putting up with my foibles over the years, have taught me a great deal of what I know today.

And finally a big thank you to you, the reader, for choosing this book. I hope you will find its contents useful and that you will find something within its pages that will make a difference to your life.

Brian Salter
Abu Dhabi
2009

01

Why should I need to learn presentation skills?

It seems to come as a surprise to many that giving an effective presentation or speech is one of the key ingredients for a successful career. For many, also, it is one of the most terrifying.

Are you one of those people for whom presenting is a necessary evil? Or even someone who will make any excuse simply to get out of it? If so, you're in good company. Millions of people the world over are willing to give it a go just so long as it is to team members or people they can call friends. As often as not, the presentation will go well, but it doesn't seem to get any easier. For many people, simply standing out from the crowd and speaking in public makes them uncomfortable, embarrassed or insecure.

But the good news is that this fear can be overcome. It's not that difficult either, and becoming a competent presenter will lead to many new opportunities, both at work and in one's private life too.

Now, just think about that for a minute. *A key skill that anyone, serious about making it big at work or in business, needs to possess is the art of being able to give a presentation.* Can that really be true?

Communication is at the heart of good leadership

One way in which individuals are evaluated for leadership roles is by assessing their ability to communicate effectively and clearly to an audience. This is because a leader or manager has constantly to communicate to his team the bigger picture, the tasks at hand, the challenges that are being faced; and the inability of a leader to convey clearly and effectively a certain message could be the difference between meeting goals and targets and not being able to do so.

So it's not an option. It's an essential professional skill that should be learned by each and every manager. Even so, some might argue that our fears are exacerbated as we become more and more used to the faceless communications of the twenty-first century. But it is something everyone can learn to love. Anyone who wants to be able to present his or her ideas to a large body of people, or simply to a room full of people, and to influence them needs to be able to face an audience and to engage with those people.

Presentation skills are not a one-size-fits-all technique

Of course, the giving of formal presentations is only part of the picture. Presentations come in many other 'flavours' as well. Simply holding meetings, or pitching to customers or potential clients – even motivating a team – requires these essential skills. Many business people spend a great deal of their working day attending one meeting after another and their ability to present their ideas is a crucial element of their success – or lack to it!

Being able to present well and to hold an audience is also a crucial factor in the way other people see you as a leader. Someone who cannot engage their audiences is unlikely to inspire those who have to follow them, however good their ideas are. If you are in line for a company promotion and there is someone else trying for the same position, whom do you think the selection committee will choose? Someone who has good ideas but finds it difficult to communicate, or someone who is comfortable inspiring others to agree with what he has to say?

Falling at the first hurdle

In my experience, just as there are many people who shy away from standing up and speaking in public, there are also many who claim to be good presenters, but whose delivery falls well short of expectations. I'm sure you can think of an instance where you had to listen to someone who burbled on for ages but who had totally lost the attention of their audience long before they reached the end of their theme.

Why was that? Where did they go wrong? How could they have improved things to have the audience on their side? We'll be returning to those key questions again and again throughout this book, but for the moment, consider the following scenario.

Case study

XYZ Widgets Ltd has a sales manual that lists a number of different rules, pricing and customer segmentation models which its sales team needs to learn by heart. (They already know that the key to a successful sale is to engage their potential clients!)

Following the launch of XYZ's latest and best widget, 50 new sales staff have been recruited to go out into the marketplace and open up new sales channels across the country. To cope with the large number of 'newbies', XYZ decides to hold a couple of induction courses at the same time, given by two different sales managers – Nick and Tony.

Nick defines his objectives as follows:

- Inform the delegates in the induction programme about the policies and procedures that they are expected to follow.

Tony's objectives are listed as:

- Based on the sales manual, get the participants to learn what is expected of them.
- Get them to understand the pricing models.
- Get them to understand the customer segmentation profiles.
- Get them to see how following the rules and regulations of the organisation will gain them new customers and thereby aid them in their career progression.

Based on their respective objectives, each presenter sets about creating their respective presentations. Nick creates a fantastic PowerPoint presentation using loads of pictures and animations.

Tony creates a presentation that employs a wide variety of tools. It has PowerPoint slides, handouts and activities – which are essentially group exercises – as well as some games in which the team will be required to participate. Each of these tools is designed to bring about specific objectives for the participants.

Much to Nick's concern, during the presentations he discovers that as the day wears on some of his delegates are beginning to fidget, and some are even starting to nod off. How could this possibly be? He is covering everything that has been asked of him and surely these young hopefuls know that they have to learn the content before they can even hope to become fully fledged members of XYZ Widget's sales team?

Tony, on the other hand, has a bunch of trainees who seem to be having a great time. Not only are they in high jinx, but they are all animatedly following the proceedings and answering all the questions that he is firing at them. Even in the 'graveyard' shift immediately following lunch, when experience shows that this is the time that concentration is least effective, Tony's trainees still seem fired up.

So what has happened? Why the difference between Tony's and Nick's groups of Widget trainees?

The answer, of course, is how the different objectives set down by the two individuals led to the creation of content that was markedly different from one another. Not only was the content different, but the way the two trainers set about meeting the desired results also differed. The presentations couldn't have been more different. And the final results – even though they were both presenting on the same topic – were consequently very different.

Tony was interested in getting people to learn, so he set objectives that kept in mind what the audience actually wanted to come away from the presentation having learned. He realised that it was what they wanted for themselves that was more important than what he wanted for himself.

Nick, on the other hand, approached the presentation from the view point of what he himself wanted. So he chose content and an approach that best suited him. The result was that he had lost his audience midway through the day.

Now, one could of course argue that the delivery style and tools employed by both were different and that made some difference to the overall results. Tony may have been a better presenter than Nick and that could have made a crucial difference. But I would argue that even if they were both presenters of the same calibre, Tony's presentation would always have had a greater impact and yielded better results, simply because of the manner in which the objectives for a presentation on the same topic, for a very similar audience, were defined. It was this that set the tone for the overall approach, the content, the tools used in the delivery and consequently the outcome of the presentation.

Tony defined the objectives of his presentation in terms of what he wanted the participants to learn. Nick, however, defined the objectives in terms of what he wanted to talk about. The results were very different.

Think of it in these terms: most of the time when you're presenting, you're actually selling an idea. You might be selling an idea to a team, or selling a service or product to a client; either way, your presentation is looking for acceptance from your target audience. It's as simple as that. And that's why presenting skills are essential regardless of whether you want to rise up the corporate ladder, be a super salesman, or lead a team. The negative side of it is that if you are bad at presenting the likelihood is that you will find that many doors are slammed in your face as you pick your way through the jungle of life!

So what can you do to overcome that fear that is inherent in so many of us – simply drying up (literally in many cases, when our mouths become dry and we desperately want to wet our lips, but find our tongues are no help whatsoever in this regard); or telling jokes that fall on deaf ears; or even forgetting what it is we were supposed to be talking about – and yes, that happens all too often when nerves take over.

I discovered recently that this phenomenon even has its own name – Katagelophobia – the fear of making fools of ourselves! Again, this is something that we will be returning to later in this book; for worry not – the good news is that even a bad attack of nerves can be overcome.

Is it possible to define what *NOT* to do?

It is often the case that a bad presenter, or someone who has never even attempted presenting before, has no idea how bad they actually are. And the first they know of this sorry state of affairs is when they get feedback from someone else that, perhaps, the presentation could have been a little better; or perhaps it is only when they have been asked to give a presentation that they realise that they have absolutely no idea where to start.

It's a bit like writing a book, I always think. How often have you heard someone tell you that they would love to write a book about their experiences, but then they come up with every lame excuse under the sun why they don't have enough time, or why others wouldn't appreciate all their effort in putting it together … or whatever. The truth, as often as not, is that they simply do not know – have never even thought about – how to set about preparing the material, getting it to flow, creating a killer opening, describing their experiences using metaphor or simile, and the 101 other things they need to have thought about when creating that best-selling book that is sitting inside their head just waiting for the chance to see the light of day!

But, before we go any further, let's consider what makes a *bad* presentation; because in some ways it is much easier to list what is common in bad presentations than to lay down the rules about what makes a good presentation.

I have sat through many presentations that left me wondering what the point of them was. Did they have a purpose? Or were the presenters simply asked to fill a time slot, irrespective of the feelings of their audiences? For without a clear purpose, any presentation is going to leave an audience listless and wishing desperately for it to end.

That negative aspect, in my experience, has to be followed closely by simply not understanding the needs of our audience. If they leave at the end of our spiel wondering why they bothered turning up in the first place, we have palpably failed. They have to go away feeling they gained some benefit from being there. Now, that must sound obvious, and of course it is. But who hasn't sat through at least one presentation which left them feeling exactly that way?

Just as important is the amount of physical preparation one takes in putting together a presentation. Lack of preparation shows all too clearly. What we are actually saying to our audience is we can't be bothered to make the effort on their behalf. And if we can't be bothered to prepare, then why should we expect them to be bothered to listen – or even to stay awake!

Tone and structure are so important

A lack of preparation has other connotations too. A badly prepared presentation will often lack the necessary structure that holds it all together, or leave an absence of a clear path that allows our audience to catch the drift of our argument. And this will often coincide with a lack of rapport building with our audience, meaning they won't be on our side wanting our presentation to succeed.

Some presenters are so engaged in their subject matter that they tend to drone on interminably, giving a delivery that is mono-tonal and thereby monotonous and virtually guaranteeing to send their audiences to sleep. I often think that some people have it easier than others in this respect. Love them or hate them, there are some accents, such as the Belfast twang for instance, that by their very nature have a sing-song timbre to them. Others – the 'Estuary' English of Essex and Kent, or the Midlander who speaks in a typical 'Brummie' accent – may have a more difficult time of it, as was shown in a survey conducted as part of the BBC Voices Project that was launched in January 2005.

Perhaps some of the tonal languages of the Far East such as Burmese or Thai or Vietnamese have it easiest as these languages are rich in polyphony. If you have ever surfed the myriad of satellite TV channels beamed into everyone's homes these days, you can find some languages that are beautiful to listen to even though you may not understand a single word!

I once attended a cultural evening way out in the desert, some 30 miles from the Saudi capital, Riyadh. There must have been some two or three hundred Saudis there, sitting on and around a swathe of carpets laid out on the sand. The highlight of the evening was about an hour's worth of poetry reading. The Arab world highly values this art form and though – at the time – I spoke hardly a word of Arabic, the performances were absolutely spell binding. The 'music' of the words, rich in timbre, and varying in pitch and speed and intimacy, beguiled the audience and at the end of the entire performance I left, with a sense of *Wow!* in the same way you might be on a high when leaving a concert or a particularly exciting film. And as we shall see later in this book, performing what you are wanting to present is an integral and intimate part of getting the audience on side and making your overall presentation highly memorable.

Building castles in the air

Another thing that we experience all too often is the 'pack of cards' syndrome – where a speaker uses weak evidence to support his ideas and the entire talk is in danger of collapse, either because the arguments don't stack up, or because the speaker loses the credibility of his audience. The moral here is simple – we must do our homework as we can bet our bottom dollar that there will almost certainly be some bright spark in the audience who is intent on showing off what he knows – at our expense!

Knowing how to set the boundaries

Not knowing when to stop is another no-no to be found in the handbook of bad presentation. If we go on too long boredom sets in and our audience will start drifting into the realms of what's for dinner tonight, or when will I see my girlfriend again, or wondering what dress to wear for next weekend's party!

And another cringe-maker, so common at wedding parties, is the use of jokes that either aren't funny, or that leave our audience stoney-faced, or are totally inappropriate for the occasion. And here I'm always reminded of that wonderful film *Four Weddings and a Funeral*. Do you remember when the upper class 'twit' listens to someone else's wedding speech and tries to emulate the same structure and stories in his own best man's speech ... and in the process fails miserably, simply because he isn't able to build the speech up in a structured way. All he is doing is using the 'best bits' which, taken out of context, are totally unrelated to one another. *If in doubt, leave 'em out* is what I tell people who come on my courses. Some people are superb joke tellers; the majority of us, however, are not!

And finally, the pièce-de-resistance – the one thing that kills more presentations than almost anything else known to man: Death by PowerPoint. Many presenters fall into the trap of having far too many slides absolutely crammed to bursting with information. If it's so important for our audience to have these facts and figures, then we should give them a handout. They are not going to remember a quarter of what they have seen in our slides and, besides, have they come all this way to hear us or to read our slides?

Again, we'll come back to this very important point later in the book; but you should know that on average, if you ask someone who has sat through a presentation – even the best presentation he has ever been to – the chances are that all he will remember are three facts from the entire session. That's right. Just three; four if they're lucky. That's true of a news bulletin on television, a talk at a society club meeting, or a company financial briefing. So, you see, there is simply no point in cramming as much information as possible into our slides.

So what are we waiting for?

So there we are. Nine things to avoid and we're well on our way to giving a successful presentation ... Well, nearly!

How about the good attributes? How, after the event, do we know – can we measure – if our presentation was a success?

For a start, did we manage to engage our audience – or were they fidgeting and staring out of the window?

Were we logical in the way we structured our data and our key messages? For that is an important key to helping people understand what it is we are trying to convey to them.

How did our visual aids come across? We have already identified the Death-by-PowerPoint syndrome, but were ours clear and uplifting?

Did we connect with our audience, keeping eye contact and talking *with* them rather than *at* them?

Were we confident, exuding exuberance and confidence in what we were saying?

Did we enunciate and project ourselves clearly?

Did we finish our presentation with a *bang*?

So, we have to learn some of the positives as well as learn what not to do. It's not difficult. Anyone can gather how to do it, and what's more we can learn to love doing it too. Presenting is a skill, just like playing the piano or driving a car. If others can learn to do it, so can we. And in the following pages we will be considering all the stages necessary on that road to success.

Summary

- Presentations come in many flavours – from holding meetings, to pitching to customers or even motivating a team.
- Being able to present well is a crucial factor in the way people see you as a leader.
- Most of the time when presenting, you are selling an idea.
- Without a clear purpose, any presentation is destined for failure.

INSTANT TIP

With a little practice, and following some of the basic do's and don'ts, anyone can become not just an OK-presenter, but a master in the art of good presentation.

02

What do I want to achieve?

The starting point for any good presentation has to be why we are doing it in the first place. Maybe someone at work has called upon us to speak about a work-related topic: how well our department is doing on a company-wide project, for instance. Or we may be giving a sales pitch to a prospective company, or giving a training presentation, or addressing a conference, or 101 other reasons for getting up on our hind legs and exposing ourselves to public scrutiny as we attempt to find *le bon mot* and have the audience eating out of our hands.

Most presentations are designed to sell an idea. And as any marketer will tell us, the art of good selling is to tie in our product or service with the interests of our buyers. So, the corollary of this is that the art of a good presentation is to tie in our messages with the interests of our audience.

Are they there to be informed or kept up to date on a fast moving marketplace? Perhaps they are there to be trained? Or to have some facet of our business explained to them? Some presentations are about building relationships, or inspiring and motivating a workforce. Perhaps we want to challenge their assumptions, or to provoke their curiosity in a particular area? We might be trying to sell them something, or getting them to buy in to our way of thinking.

At the end of the day, the main reason to present to anyone is to change something. It might be we want to change the way they think about something; or their behaviour in regard to a specific issue. Whatever the reason for our performance, the basic approach we need to take is pretty much the same. The way we present ourselves, the way we control our voice, the way we structure content and the way we put our points across to the audience are basic skills that can be learned and put to good effect.

What will change from presentation to presentation, however, is the way we target our messages at the audiences concerned. The types of visual aids used and the level at which we are pitching also need to be targeted in the right way to the people to whom we are presenting.

For, as we have seen, it comes as no surprise that a large part of the success of our presentation will depend on whether we can match the expectations of both the organiser of the event and the audience who have taken time out to come to listen to us. If we don't meet their expectations, then it doesn't matter how wonderful our theme is, the fact is that we will have failed!

Analysing the event

Knowing what it is we are being asked to speak about is only one small part of preparing for the occasion. Why are we there? What is the objective of us speaking at all? Are we simply there to fill time? Hopefully this is not the case. Yet so many presenters fall into this most basic of traps. They are asked to talk about widgets and they do so – interminably. But they have never bothered to find out what it is about widgets the audience wants to know. So they drone on in their own little world, looking at widgets from their own perspective, and wonder why half-way through they have totally lost the concentration of their audience.

So before we can even begin to think about what our presentation will contain, we need some basic answers to some equally basic questions:

- What organisation is holding this event and what are its objectives?
- What does the organiser hope to achieve by asking us to speak?
- What ground does he want us to cover?
- How much time has he earmarked for us to speak?
- What other speakers are being asked to present?
- And how will our talk tie in with what they have to say?

There are other equally important questions that need to be asked that will help us tailor our presentation to the particular event:

- What is the nature of this particular occasion?
- How formal is it?
- Is there to be a chairman for the session?
- What clothes should we wear?
- Will there be a question and answer session at the end?
- Will there be a panel discussion following?

And perhaps the most important – since we have already seen that meeting the delegates' expectations is paramount to our success – how will we be able to meet their expectations?

Understanding our audience

We may well have the best data, and have prepared a killer performance. We may well be the best speaker on the planet; but if we do not tailor-make the presentation to our audience, then all this will be for nothing.

Our primary task, therefore, is to understand where they are coming from; we need to identify their objectives and work out how best we can fit in with their aims in the context in which we are participating. We are endeavouring to fit in the benefits of our subject matter to the audience's areas of interest. By analysing our listeners, we can then best decide how to present our ideas.

Putting it simply, it is our audience who should be the centre of our attention. It is they who must feel satisfied at the end, otherwise why are we bothering in the first place?

So the following questions must be asked and the answers understood before we can even begin to put together the content of what we want to say.

Firstly, why is the audience being assembled at all? What common background brings them together? It may be they are professionals working in the same discipline; they may have shared values; or have a common interest in our topic; or – and one has to face the possibility – they have been delegated to be there and don't really know why they are there at all!

However, let us assume that they are willing participants. In which case, what is their level of expertise? How much do they know about our topic? And how experienced are they themselves? After all, it may be that they are experts in their own right and that we are talking to people on our own level; equally they may know little about the subject – in which case we have to pitch our presentation at a lower level so as not to lose their attention. This will also be impacted by their general level of education or sophistication.

OK. We have found out who our audience is and their level of knowledge in the subject matter. So why are they there? What do they want to glean from our presentation? Do they want to pick up new thought processes and information from us? Do they want to be stimulated with new ideas? Do they want to learn about practical techniques in their areas of expertise? Do they want entertaining? Or a combination of all these things?

I remember a few years ago being asked to give a presentation to a group of employees working in a 'dot com' company. They knew their subject matter inside out. There was no way I could even begin to compete with the knowledge they already had in their areas of expertise. What the organisers wanted, however, was to give them a break from work and get the message through to them that, as they were at the very forefront of technology, there were no preset rules that they could follow. They had to think outside the box and think the unthinkable.

To be successful they needed to think through the what-if questions, rather than what had already been done. So my theme concentrated on gazing into the future; contemplating some of the major advances that were already being worked on in R&D labs throughout the world and throwing out ideas, some of which seemed extremely far-fetched, yet stimulated the audience into thinking that maybe some of their own ideas weren't so 'wacky' and impossible to achieve. Interestingly enough, quite a few of those wacky ideas are now firmly embedded in the marketplace.

How receptive is our audience to ideas?

While contemplating our audience, we also need to ask about their general attitude to what is going on. Will they be open-minded and curious about the subject matter? Or hostile and sceptical? Above all, will they be supportive and interested in what is being discussed? In my experience there is nothing worse than standing up in front of a group of people who really don't want to be there at all or who are hostile from the very start.

I once had to face precisely this situation when presenting to a group of around 20 people why some three-quarters of them were to be made redundant. The company had been going through a rough patch and was ripe for a hostile takeover. My department was seen as an easy culling area and the only thing that got me through the presentation was the fact that I would be one of those on the redundancy list! It was a bitter-sweet experience and one I would hope never to have to repeat! Interestingly, those who gave most problems during the presentation were the ones whose jobs were secure – for the moment – rather than the unfortunates who were being shown the door; a classic case, I think, of fear of uncertainty making itself felt.

It can also be useful to find out the general characteristics of our audience. What is their age range and their general degree of diversity? And especially important, I believe – what is the ratio of male to female? This last point might seem a little controversial to some but it has been shown in a number of scientific experiments that the way men and women think is markedly different. It's all to do with which sides of the brain we use to gather and process information. Experiments have shown that men tend to be much more single-track-minded than women, who find it much easier to think laterally.

Many would argue that this is part of life's natural evolution – the male of the species was the hunter-gatherer whose main concentration and raison d'être was to provide food for the family; whilst the females, who had to look after the kids, do the cooking and all the other household duties, had by necessity to be able to think a number of parallel thoughts such as whether the supper was about to burn, were the children safe, did the fire need another log?

I well remember one guy I knew, whose identity is probably best not revealed, whose routine when making breakfast was to put on the kettle and then wait for it to boil; at which point he opened the cupboard, took out the coffee mugs, poured the coffee into the mugs and then the water on top of that. Now with the coffee successfully made, he took the bread out of the fridge and placed the requisite number of slices in the toaster and waited for it to pop up, after which he would go to the fridge look for the butter, spread the toast, put the butter back, go get the jam, spread the toast, put the jam back and then start thinking about preparing the poached eggs or porridge or whatever. And so it went on. To say it was painful to have to watch would be an understatement; yet this guy was a brilliant computer whiz kid who could work out complex problems in a long computer algorithm. I guess it was just another example of Darwin's theories of evolution in action!

Of course, that is a huge generalisation and there are always major exceptions. But women are generally better at multitasking and do find it easier to process seemingly unrelated topics at the same time. And this could therefore have a bearing on the way we present our information.

And a final thought about audiences. What kind of presentations are they accustomed to? Is group participation encouraged? Do they expect handouts or visual aids? And what are their expectations on formality and variety? Sometimes it pays to provide exactly what they are expecting. At other times we can shock and thereby grab their attention if we present in a totally unconventional way.

And sometimes that decision is forced upon us, as I remember all too well when I was asked to present to some company sales staff who had been assigned to take part in a team-building weekend. The theme was advertising using the internet and I had been asked to talk to them in the evening so that they had time to mull over what I had said before the following day's sessions. The team building involved competing in groups of three getting from A to B across open countryside. Unfortunately the organisers had totally failed to prepare for the torrential rain that struck in the afternoon. By the time the delegates had arrived at the country hotel which was their destination, they were like a pack of drowned rats.

It was decided to delay dinner while they all went for hot showers and thereafter the bar was thrown open before the meal. Again, what the organisers in their generosity had failed to think about was that a free bar for some 20 young sales staff could have unwanted side effects! By the time they came to dinner, some of them were definitely the worse for drink, to the point where mashed potato was being thrown liberally across the dining hall in a food fight.

Obviously any serious presentation would have been impossible to give under these circumstances. But on the basis of 'knowing your audience' I was able to make last-minute changes to my theme, likening viral advertising on the web to their behaviour during dinner when one person threw the first fistful of mashed potato, which resulted in more mashed potato being thrown about, which in turn resulted in mashed potato flying across the whole room.

In retrospect it was probably one of the best presentations I ever gave, though not one I could easily have prepared for if I had had a little more time to think about it!

How can NLP techniques help our presentation?

NLP stands for Neuro Linguistic Programming. The science of NLP was developed by a cyberneticist in the 1970s working in tandem with a professor of linguistics. Together they attempted to discover if there was a common thread shown by people who exhibited excellence in their chosen fields. The results of their research created a model that identified essential thoughts, feelings and beliefs when reflected in these people's success.

Obviously a treatise on the use of NLP would be inappropriate in this book, but for further reading on this most fascinating of subjects, look no further than Mo Shapiro's excellent treatise in this CMI *Instant Manager* series.

Using the NLP approach, we can imagine ourselves in other people's positions, looking at a scenario through their eyes, rather than just from our one position.

Apart, then, from our own perspective, we can put ourselves in the shoes of our audience and imagine how we would react if we had to listen to ourselves talking about our own pet subject. How would we, sitting at the back of the hall, react to our voice, to our mannerisms, to the size of the font on our slides?

We could also put ourselves in a neutral position, looking at both our audience and ourselves, but as a third party observer – a bit like a proverbial fly on the wall. In this way we could examine the relationships that are developing between ourselves, the speaker, and our audience on the receiving end.

How does location affect the presentation?

Just as it is important to understand our audience and their needs, so too must we do our research on where we are being asked to perform; for the actual location can have a big bearing on the outcome of the presentation.

The size of room can be a critical factor, since if the room is too big we will lose any feeling of intimacy that is an important element of successful presentation – as we will see later in this book. So, too, will there be a danger that our voice will struggle to be heard at the back of the room. Much better that we – or preferably the organiser – moves everyone to the front so that we can make up a small grouping, regardless of how big the auditorium actually is.

It is always best to visit the location and actual room or hall at an early stage if at all possible. As the military always say: *time spent on reconnaissance is never wasted*. The last thing we want is a nasty surprise when we are least expecting it.

At this time, we should also check out the equipment available rather than leave to chance that there will be, for example, the right type of projector, or whether microphones will be supplied. Lighting, too, can be gauged since this often can play a vital role in the success or failure of a presentation.

Answers we should also ascertain at this 'recce' should include:

- How long will it take me to reach the destination and is there plenty of parking – we should always leave plenty of time before a performance. Much better to be far too early than even a few minutes late.
- Where will I sit prior to and after my performance? I find it amazing that organisers regularly forget to include an extra chair for their star guest!
- Do I speak from a platform? It's usually better if we can be slightly higher than our audience in order to facilitate eye contact.
- Is there a podium or rostrum, or will I have a table on which to place my notes and visual aids?
- How will the audience be seated? Around tables or in rows? And has the organiser thought through what is the best seating layout? (Very often it is the way the venue has decided to place the tables and chairs, rather than the organiser's choice.)
- What are the acoustics like? Will I need a microphone and if so who will control the volume?
- Will there be a flip chart, computer projection, DVD or VHS playback facilities?
- Where are the power sockets, should I need to plug in my own equipment?

So how do we actually define our objectives?

We've spoken to the organiser, and analysed our audience make up. We've done a recce of the speech venue; but we still haven't tackled the most important question of all. What is our objective? Having got answers to the earlier questions, we are now in a much better position to formalise what it is we are trying to achieve.

We may have been asked to speak on a particular subject in which we are expert. But why? Is it to give a background introduction to the subject? Or to describe our latest research findings?

Our objectives will include the overall components of which we may wish to avail ourselves. The methods we use will be determined later. And hereby is an important difference. We mustn't at this stage be sidetracked as to how we are going to deliver our message. The content and overall reasons for our performing in the first place are what we are considering right now.

Remember that there may be things we might wish to hide (such as commercially confidential information) and there may be hidden personal agendas that we also have (could it be that we wish to show the CEO that he has an excellent member of staff on his team?).

In reality we will be seeking to achieve a number of objectives, some of which may include:

- Informing and updating our audience on what has been happening within our own department or organisation.

- Explaining or defending a position we have taken such as a price rise or disappointing sales figures.
- Selling a product or service – whether this is to potential customers, or perhaps to journalists in a news conference.
- Training or educating people to develop their skills or understanding.
- Building relationships whereby we are using the presentation event as a get-to-know-you exercise.
- Influencing and winning support as well as changing attitudes.
- Raising our profile not just within the company but throughout the profession.
- Inspiring others to perform or perhaps simply to say 'thank you for your efforts'.

Put simply, without being able to define what it is we are trying to achieve will doom our presentation to failure before we have even begun. Arguments that appear to benefit the audience in some way will be much more likely to succeed than those which only appeal to us. They may not actually agree with what we are saying, but if we give them something to think about and tell it with confidence, enthusiasm and integrity, then we are well on the way to achieving our objectives.

So, throughout the entire process, what we must never forget is to put ourselves in the audience's position. We should never ask ourselves, 'what do we want to say?' but rather, 'what do we want them to hear?' There is a fine and subtle distinction here. What we are trying to achieve is a particular behaviour we would like our audience to exhibit after our presentation, be that changes in behavioural patterns, or an understanding of a particular topic, or a willingness to accept new targets, or whatever.

People in the PR business call this *key messaging*. I am reminded of that famous cartoon in which a man is talking to his dog. 'OK Rover,' he says; 'now you stay out of the garbage! You understand, Rover? Stay out of the garbage or else!' And the poor mutt, who isn't quite on the same wavelength as his master, simply hears 'Blah blah Rover; blah blah blah blah blah blah blah Rover. blah blah blah blah blah blah blah'.

So a PR person would tell you to determine what issues are important to your customers, employees, allies and other audiences; decide which issues are negative or positive; develop positive responses for negative issues; craft messages for specific audiences; simplify statements – eliminate jargon; craft in terms laypersons can understand.

American presentation gurus use what they call the elevator test. This exercise requires you to sell your key message in 30 to 45 seconds. Imagine you are riding up to the executive floor and in steps the company chairman. 'I'm in a hurry,' he explains apologetically. 'Just run me through the key points will you?' Well, could you wrap up the key fundamental points of your presentation before you reach that top floor?

Maybe you think such a scenario is unlikely. Yet it is extremely common to be asked to cut one's presentation from 20 minutes to ten minutes or from an hour to half an hour. Could you do it at a moment's notice? Whether you will need to in reality is not the point. Being able to do so will help you tighten your overall message and help you to be clearer in the process.

The good news is that we will be examining all of these aspects in more detail as we move on through this book.

Summary

- High-impact presentations are designed to address the needs and expectations of an audience.
- To understand what we need to include in our presentation we need first to ascertain why the event is being held, what are the expectations of the audience and what are the key messages we are trying to put across.
- It is a useful exercise to put ourselves in the position of our audience and imagine how we would react if having to listen to ourselves.
- The location and venue can both play their part in the success of a presentation.

INSTANT TIP

The clearer we can understand what it is we are trying to achieve, the better able we will be to craft a powerful presentation around it.

03

How do I best put together my presentation?

We've laid out the objectives of our presentation and we have a fair idea of the make up of our audience and what they will expect as payback for giving up their time to come and listen to us. So the next thing we must consider is what is going to be included in the content.

That probably seems quite obvious. We're going to be talking about the subject in hand and imparting our insight into that particular subject area.

But how do we start? What do we include? And equally as important, what do we leave out? And how should we structure the presentation itself? For it is not until we try to put our thoughts down into a logical sequence that we find it is not as easy as we might at first believe.

Sourcing and manipulating our data

So let's get down to the basics. Where will we get our information from in the first place? We may already be an authority on the subject matter. Perhaps we've written an article on it, or undertaken some detailed research. Or perhaps someone else has already done that research and has given us permission to use it in our material.

Whatever the expertise we already have in our subject matter, though, the sooner we start actually to think about the content the better. For that way it embeds itself into our subconscious rather than allowing the information to be crammed into our brains just days or, worse still, hours before we have to deliver.

I find that some of my best quality thinking time is around 3 o'clock in the morning. The thought patterns go round and round in my brain without my even realising it until I wake up in the middle of the night with, literally, a brain wave. I even have a pad of paper by my bedside to record that 'moment of truth', because otherwise I just know that come the morning I will have forgotten it once again.

I also drive around the Middle East with a little dictation recorder in my car that I can use to jot down my wild thoughts as I'm chuntering along some desert road! (Of course, I wouldn't dream of doing this in the UK where it is against the law to use a dictation machine while driving according to the legislation regarding mobile phones and similar devices that is common across much of Europe – not that there are many desert roads along which to chunter in this part of the world!)

During sleeping hours, or at other times when our brains have a breather from having to think as 'we go into autopilot', they try to unclutter the mass of information gleaned during our waking hours, 'throwing out the garbage' and putting things into order and perspective.

Now, that might simply be a reflection of my untidy thoughts, but whether you're a logical, methodical thinker, or you have thoughts that come at you from all directions, try the pencil-and-paper-by-the-bedside routine, or have some other handy way of jotting down your thoughts. It will almost certainly help.

Another reason for starting early into our research is that it gives us time to query what we have found and this might in turn lead to new approaches that we might not even have thought about. If we leave our information gathering to the last minute, we simply don't have this luxury.

There's an old saying: to use one source of information for our work is out-and-out plagiarism. To use a number of sources is called research! But why would we want to plagiarise someone else's work anyway? Our audience might just as well be given the source material and be told to go away and read it for themselves. And anyway, the world is stuffed full of data. On most subject matter, there is no shortage of information, especially now we live in the internet age.

As often as not, the question is not *where* can I search for information, but how on earth can I wade through so much that is available? For, apart from the internet, there are books, magazine articles, our own experiences or research, those of our colleagues and friends, and a host of other sources.

When it's cuil to use google

For my part, I find that spending half an hour to an hour with Google, Cuil or a similar-calibre search engine on the web throws up all kinds of ideas on almost every subject under the sun – certainly enough to lead me off onto various tracks that I might not even have thought about.

There are also online repositories of information that give a useful overview of a particular subject – wikipedia.org, of course, comes to mind in this regard – and again this can be useful in shaping our own thoughts, giving pointers to new material we might not even have considered up until this point. But a word of warning: much of the information on the web that is available for free is unsubstantiated. So don't just believe everything you read. Try to check out the information you find there with a more authoritative source such as a trade journal.

In this respect, the newer encyclopaedic site knol.google.com takes the Wikipedia experience one stage further by listing the sources of the information presented and firmly apportioning it to individuals who take responsibility for the information they have added, as opposed to Wikipedia's policy of allowing anyone to update or change the information.

Filtering the information

As we can very easily end up with far too much information, I tend to have a number of text documents open on my PC (such as created by notebook.exe, which has the added advantage that it strips out any formatting making the whole thing easier to read), and copy and paste information from the web into the different documents which deal with different aspects of the particular subject matter in hand. (Though if the source of the information is essential to know, then I always record the website from which it was derived.)

By incorporating information from a number of sources into one text document, and keeping individual themes in different text documents, I find that I can structure my thought processes much better than if I were, for instance, simply to save each and every page load of information as a standard html document. But everyone thinks and works in different ways. If this isn't representative of the way your thought processes work, then find a method with which you are comfortable.

Clarifying our thoughts is the name of the game here. We could find it useful to create a spider diagram – what the famous work psychologist Professor Edward de Bono termed a 'mind map'. It works by entering a central idea into a circle in the centre of a page. From this circle lines radiate to other circles with ideas that are linked to that central theme in some way. And each of these circles has links to other idea bubbles, and so on. Some people find it useful to have separate colours for different themes or parts of the overall presentation, but that is not really necessary. The idea is that you can brainstorm ideas and keep on entering them into linked circles and literally get a map of your thought processes.

From this visual presentation you can see at a glance if your brainstorming has covered all the areas in enough detail; or if you have too much detail on any one aspect at the expense of others.

You can even get software these days for creating the diagrams, which can be extremely useful and a great time saver when you have loads of ideas and have simply run out of paper! Also, you can easily switch the placement of different circles without having to redraw the diagram each time.

One bonus of using spider diagrams is that it forces us to enter the information into a structure as we go along. It's a very powerful technique and, especially when we are faced with giving long presentations, it is an invaluable tool.

One often neglected source of information and data can come from within. Brainstorming either by ourselves or with others is invaluable. We should write down all the thoughts that spring into our mind regardless of whether at this moment in time we consider them valuable or trivial. Examples, anecdotes, passing what-if thoughts, anything at all; write it all down. We can select and reject the content later when we have had time to digest it.

The main thing to aim for, however, is not to overload ourselves with too much information, which is so easy to do. Those new to giving presentations tend to save far too much because they are afraid they will run out of things to say. And then when it comes to sorting out the wheat from the chaff – getting rid of the inconsequential material – they have a real problem on their hands.

Another error, made by many, is to use material that has been used before in the mistaken belief that if it served the purpose the last time around, it can be repeated on this occasion. But think back to what we talked about in the last chapter. Every audience is different; it has different needs, different aspirations, has a different make up, is listening under different conditions... So it is hardly likely that what worked for one audience is going to have exactly the same effect on another. By all means use it as useful research, if that is what it is. But if we reuse some of it, we must do so because it has earned its place in our presentation on its own merits.

How do I structure the presentation?

The hardest part for many people putting together a talk or a presentation is where to start. How do I kick off? How can I grab the audience's attention? And what about the overall structure?

It may be appropriate to give our audience a little bit of background information about ourselves; though if this is an organised event, rather than giving a presentation to work colleagues, for example, this should not really be necessary if the MD or organiser has done his or her job properly. And anyway, it may simply make us out to have an ego problem. Sure, it is useful to let the audience know why we have the experience and qualifications to be talking to them; but if they don't know this by the time we start, then perhaps something has been missing in the initial set up of the event anyway?

It is also a pretty boring way to open any presentation. I mean, consider:

Hello. My name is Brian Salter and today I'm going to talk to you about widgets. My background in widget production goes back to the days when I was a graduate trainee in XYZ Widgets Ltd and I worked my way up the widget ladder until I got where I am today ... head of widget production ...

(Are you asleep yet?)

It can be useful, however, to remind our audience why *they* are there in the first place. By reminding them of the objective of the presentation we can neatly put everything into context so everyone starts off from the same point of comprehension. Sometimes, of course, this would be totally inappropriate if, say, we were trying to change behaviour patterns and we wanted to guide the delegates into making that inference for themselves. But for many presentations, by stating our objective at the start, the audience knows what is in it for them.

To help us in this regard, there are a number of tried and tested methods. If the presentation is to be formal, one in which we want to impart important knowledge, then we simply cannot beat a formal structure in which we tell our audience what we are going to talk about, we then tell them what it is we want them to learn and understand, and then we give a summary of what we have just told them.

This is the old 'Tell 'em times three' formula:

- Tell 'em what you're going to tell 'em.
- Tell 'em what you tell 'em.
- Tell 'em what you have just told 'em.

It is, of course, pretty simplistic, but to a certain degree it does work. It might appear to be overkill but it's a fact that the vast majority of people remember very little of what they have been told once; but if we give them due warning about what they are going to hear, their cognitive processes kick into action, they recognise the information that they have now come to expect, and they retain more of what they have just learned. By then reiterating a summary of what they have just heard, we can ram that information home with a pretty good chance that they will have remembered a large part of what we have just told them.

A very much less successful method of imparting information is to use what can be regarded as a logical sequence. If A, then B; and if B, then we can expect C; this has implications for D; while it may also affect E and F … and so on.

While this might be fine if we are presenting in a court of law, the chances are that our audience will fall fast asleep, or at the very least their minds will wander off into fresh pastures.

Another method of structuring a presentation is to tell it like a story. This was the sound advice given to me many years ago by a seasoned BBC professional. 'Tell it like it is,' she used to say to me. 'Tell them a story. Every story has a beginning, a middle and an end. Start at the beginning, work your way through the body of what you want to say and then give them something to remember your programme by at the end. And that way they will always come back for more.'

Perhaps she was simply summing up what Scheherezade managed to achieve all those years ago in the *Arabian Nights*. But she was right. Every presentation needs a structure, and if we follow the golden 'Scheherezade' rule, we simply cannot go wrong.

Because the human brain is very good at making comparisons and linkages to like-minded subjects, putting a presentation into a narrative structure usually holds the attention of an audience, just so long as it is relevant to the overall theme of the presentation, and just so long as we are good at telling stories in the first place. Even if we cannot structure the whole presentation into one overarching story, we can still use this method for specific parts of the talk – and we'll be looking at ways of doing this later on.

Where do I start?

It always helps when giving a talk to be a bit of a thespian. Almost every presentation benefits from a little drama added to the proceedings. To grab the audience's attention, the opening is the most crucial part. Lose our audience now and we will have a very difficult time of it trying to win them over to our side once again.

Some people start off by telling a joke, which is fine just so long as our audience hasn't heard it many times before, it is relevant to our subject matter and is well told. The problem is that the majority of us are not good at telling jokes. And if the joke falls flat, for whatever reason, it can even do more damage than good.

Worse still is to tell a joke that can offend – perhaps because of religious, cultural or sexist reasons. This could happen if we have not paid enough regard to the make up of our audience – as I witnessed on one extremely embarrassing occasion when a western diplomat referred to some of his best Scotch whisky when speaking to a group of high-ranking governmental VIPs who happened to be Muslim, describing it as 'our equivalent of your zam-zam water'. (Zam-zam is the holy spring water in Makkah, revered by pilgrims on the Haj and Umrah.) There was an intense silence that filled the room following this 'joke' during which you could have heard a proverbial pin drop.

An anecdote is another, somewhat easier way of getting attention, though admittedly not as effective as a well-told joke. The CEO of an organisation for which I used to undertake work invariably started off by telling about the good old days when his great-grandfather used to sit in church every Sunday. He would lay out on the pew in front of him a row of pennies that were visible to the preacher in the pulpit. As the sermon churned on remorselessly, he would remove the pennies one by one, and whatever was left over at the end of the sermon would be dropped loudly into the collection tray as it was passed around at the end of the service. The implication was clear. The preacher had better get a move on. The CEO was able to link that situation with the fact that his audience had glasses of wine in front of them. For their own good, he had better not talk too long, or they would not be in a suitable condition to stay awake or even make their way home at the end.

It didn't matter what the CEO was talking about. Everyone in the audience could relate to having sat through boring presentations before; and the fact that he was able to laugh at himself helped him to win over the delegates. (However, the fact that he tended to use this story over and over again meant that, invariably, there were people in his audience who eventually knew what was coming. It caused a huge amount of hilarity on one occasion when a delegate finished the story for him, and he had to learn a new story for his future speeches!)

Another way of grabbing attention is to make a controversial statement. Whether it is something we actually believe, or an idea we put forward so that, once we have shocked the audience, we can shoot it down, the effect is the same. By raising emotions, the audience is suddenly awake to our every word!

For instance, we might begin by saying, 'Today, I'm going to explain to you how we can double sales and halve costs in the next 18 months.' A bold statement indeed, and one that will have the audience hanging onto our words, if only to be able to shoot us down in flames when it comes to the Question and Answer session later on.

Yet another method of focusing our audience is to do what Haydn did with his Surprise Symphony. The music starts with a gentle theme, a lyrical melody that lulls the audience into a calm state as they contemplate the pleasant tune and drift off into whatever reveries they may have enjoyed when they have sat through other, similar pieces. The music continues at *mezzo-forte*, the audience is lulled into a state of false security and then suddenly, without any warning whatsoever, the orchestra blasts out at *triple-forte* and wakes everyone out of their slumbers. Except, of course, we don't want our audience to be drifting off during our talk; but the principle can be used to great effect.

Take the occasion, for instance, when a certain computer company – now defunct – was unveiling a new model in its range of desktop computers to members of the press. They had hired a room in a hotel in 'silicon valley' on the busy M4 corridor to the west of London. The hacks had seen it all before of course. You've seen one computer unveiling, you've seen them all; or so they thought.

'How should we grab their attention?', worried members of the company's marketing department. Eventually the answer was as simple as it was obvious. As the PC was unveiled, they would use a loud thunder flash, as used in theatres, a smoke generator would puff away with red and blue lights flashing round the room, and the PC would appear through the smoke making a dramatic appearance.

Perfect. Except for one thing. No one had checked the idea out with the hotel management beforehand. If they had, it might have been possible to have averted what happened next. As the thunder flash was set off, and the smoke generator went into action, so too did the hotel's sprinkler system! The launch of the PC was highly memorable, though not in the way it had been planned. Mind you, the press coverage given to the launch could not have been better, if you measure it purely in the number of column inches given in the papers. Well, they say there is no such thing as bad publicity and in this case the particular computer was remembered long after its day, purely for the send-off it was given at its launch, and for the fact that it was witnessed by a roomful of sodden journalists!

Can you imagine that scene? The dripping journalists? The red faces of the marketing department? Can you? Because that is another excellent way of opening up our presentation. If we invite the audience to visualise a particular experience, we are straight away transporting them into another world; and so already they are listening intently to what we are talking about. Just imagine that!

Another example is to rouse the audience's curiosity. Once, when talking to a group of airline executives, I 'set up' the room before the presentation, before my audience arrived, by placing a boiled sweet on every chair. Not surprisingly this got the delegates wondering what on earth they were meant to do with it. Should they eat it, or put it in their pockets or pretend they hadn't seen it and simply sit on it? I began my talk by making an analogy with the sweets still given out to passengers on some airlines just before taxiing to the runway. My presentation was just about to take off, I told them, so they were welcome to suck away if they wanted to enjoy the ride! All could relate to the boiled sweet experience, it certainly broke the ice when I invited the delegates to suck their sweets as I talked, and I had certainly grabbed their attention!

Yet another way of opening a presentation is to start with an analogy. '"Fire in the lake" is how the Chinese write the word for Revolution. But my talk today is about evolution, not revolution ...'

Or we could bring in the 'aaaah' factor, as in 'A true friend is someone who reaches out for your hand and touches your heart'; or the 'wow' factor, as in 'Did you know an ant can lift 50 times its own weight, can pull 30 times its own weight and always falls over on its right side when intoxicated?'

Moving into the main section

So, having engaged our audience in whatever way is most appropriate, we can now 'tell them what we are going to tell them', if that is our plan of action; or else we can move into the main theme of the presentation itself.

But, to reiterate: it's a well-researched fact that most people remember very few new ideas thrown in their direction. A media study group at Glasgow University a few years ago undertook some research on how much of the previous night's main news bulletin was remembered by their interviewees. The majority were only able to remember the subject matter of three items in a half-hour bulletin unaided. When prompted, that number rose to five items.

Interestingly, another research study conducted in India found that whereas message retention of a straightforward oral presentation amounted to only 10 per cent three days after the event, those presentations using a visual medium along with the spoken word increased audience retention to around 65 per cent of the overall content. (This is not true for everyone, as different people use different thinking styles with which to process information. For a more detailed treatise on this, you cannot do better than refer to Mo Shapiro's *Neuro Linguistic Programming* tome in this *Instant Manager* series.) We will be looking at the use of visual aids in more detail in Chapter 5.

Unlike a reader who can pause for a moment to consider the meaning behind a phrase or statement, someone who can only *listen* to us cannot pause to reconsider something that didn't quite come across the first time around. He can either choose to think over what he has just heard, or try to keep up with our voice, but he can not be expected to do both at the same time. So this gives us a special responsibility to keep our audience with us from the start right through to the very end of our presentation.

So it is simply no good throwing endless facts and figures at our delegates and expecting them to take them all on board. True, we can 'up the ante' a little by having prompts on slides (we'll come on to this later), but we shouldn't even contemplate having more than around half a dozen headings within our presentation. All the sections must follow on smoothly, one after another, in a segued sequence, leading the audience by the hand and guiding them to where we want their thought processes to go.

Data pitfalls

Many people try to avoid giving figures in their presentations, perhaps mindful of the old adage of there being 'lies, damned lies and statistics'. Yet figures are usually essential in making a business case and if you can show how your figures are arrived at, then many audiences will normally accept these at face value.

The problem comes when quoting figures out of context. If you were to say to a financial analyst, or someone who is used to dealing in shares and foreign exchange, that the FTSE100 had closed the day to stand at 5650, or that the Nikkei-Dow slumped to 11,609, that would make sense, but it might not mean an awful lot to many other people. Tell your audience, though, that the Footsie had gained four per cent that day and now this figure can be understood by most people.

It's a bit like with the weather forecasts. It is many years since the UK switched over to general use of Celcius temperatures. All the TV weather bulletins use °C – yet one can almost guarantee that in the summer months when the days are getting longer and warmer, some Fleet Street hack will run a headline along the lines of 'Temperatures in the 80s'. No matter that the vast majority of the British public would no longer be able to tell you that 15°C is the same as 60°F. The point is, it *sounds* good.

The same is true with gallons and litres. It wasn't really so long ago that British petrol stations sold fuel in gallons. Is it cynical to believe that the switch over to selling it in litres had anything to do with the sharp rise in fuel prices following the 1970s oil crisis?

How much more embarrassing would it be for a government of whatever persuasion to acknowledge that petrol now costs in the order of £4.50 per gallon than around £1 per litre?

And in Saudi Arabia, where water retails at around twice the cost of petrol, how much impact would it give to tell someone that one of the first acts of King Abdullah bin Abdulaziz on his accession was to halve the price of petrol at the pumps, as opposed to saying it was reduced to around 6p per litre?

So putting the figures into context is extremely important in a presentation. To impress an audience with figures it is important that they have something to compare them with. If sales have risen by 10 per cent over the past month, should we be impressed or not? Without knowing that the previous four months had each shown a rise of over 20 per cent, this might have looked good. Show our audience the figures in context, and they can make up their own minds.

Or can they? If we present them with a table of monthly sales that looks like this, how useful is it?

Jan	Feb	Mar	Apr	May	Jun	Jul	Aug	Sep	Oct	Nov	Dec
87	46	58	93	59	44	78	29	65	84	93	54

Figure 3.1

But present this as a pie chart …

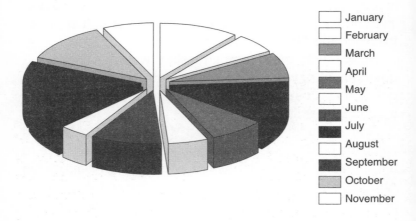

Figure 3.2

or better still as a bar chart …

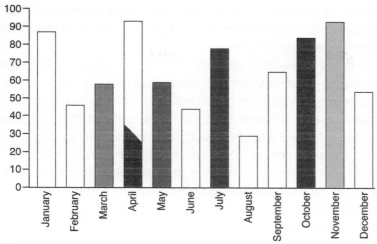

Figure 3.3

... and suddenly those figures are shown in context and become easier to fathom.

And, as we have seen above, the type of graph can also help or hinder our comprehension. For instance, a line graph is excellent for showing individual snapshots of continuous data. For discontinuous data, a bar chart is easier to understand. Vertical bar charts should be used to show changes in quantity over time; horizontal bar charts are good for comparing quantities such as varying sales figures. A stacked bar chart is useful for showing the breakdown between individual elements in overall performance; while a pie chart is useful for showing comparative data at a single point in time.

The pie chart is one of those most preferred by sales and marketing people. It has an excellent visual impact and – along the earlier lines of damned lies and statistics

– can be altered to show almost anything one wants it to show, which is probably why scientists much prefer line graphs and bar charts.

As we have said already, this is a crucial element in knowing our audience and presenting the data accordingly! We have to remember what the presentation is about and to keep going back to the reasons we are doing it. If we feel that our talk is wandering off in a tangential direction, then we need to reiterate the main points since the likelihood is that our audience may well need reminding too! Long lists of figures are never going to get an audience excited, so we should always attempt to find other ways to illustrate what we are saying.

Winding down

As we approach the close, we should summarise the main points covered in our presentation. This gives us the chance to jog the delegates' memories about all the key points we have covered. If you like, it can be regarded as a snapshot of the entire presentation.

And finally, we need to make a memorable ending. That doesn't mean necessarily surprising our delegates or letting off a thunder flash, or the like. But we should be able to round off into a comfortable close, whether that means turning the whole talk round to face the main point we opened with, or posing a question that we would like our audience to part with, or even throwing out a challenge or a call to action.

What we must not do is to end with a whimper. And that includes one of the most common and dreadful ways of ending that goes something along the lines of, *'Well, ladies and gentlemen; that's all I wanted to cover today. Are there any questions?'* It almost guarantees a slide into mediocrity, however brilliant the rest of the presentation has been.

Selecting what we are going to say

The key to allocating time to each section of a presentation is to give each of those main points enough to get our message across, but to leave enough time for the other parts in order to let the delivery flow.

Say that we are giving a talk about widgets and that we have been given half an hour for our slot. We might decide that there are four key points we wish to get across, as well as giving our killer opening and closing. So we could allocate five minutes to each section and everything would be covered.

Well, we could do it that way, but it's unlikely we could hold our audience for a full five minutes at the start simply 'warming them up'. And wouldn't that time be better spent in imparting our key messages? Why are we talking after all? As a piece of entertainment, or to put forward some ideas for consideration?

One thing to be wary of here: we should always be careful to differentiate between what it is we want to say and what it is we want to talk about. The latter might include 'our company is making excellent profits' but the key message – what it is we want to say – could be 'by giving excellent customer service that is second to none, we will improve profits further'. In other words, it is not enough simply to talk around the subject (and how boring would that be anyway?). No; we must focus on what we want our audience to take away from our presentation, and that means giving them a course of action we wish them to follow as a result of this exercise.

Perhaps we could warm the audience up with a two-minute introduction. The ending might be worth four minutes if we want to reiterate some of the key points. The two main key points might now each be allocated an extra two minutes, making seven minutes in total for each of them.

This fine-tuning approach takes discipline and focus, but it is when we concentrate on minutiae such as this that we will be able to give the most successful talk we can.

Some people find it helpful to draw a line chart divided into two-minute segments. They then allocate individual aspects of their speech to particular parts of the chart so that they have a pictorial representation of what they will deliver. It's a bit like a 'Gantt' chart in a project management study, except that, here, each segment represents specific points to be raised in the presentation.

2	2	2	2	2	2	2	2	2	2	2	2	2	2
Opening	Point 1>>		Point 2>>>>>>			Point 3>>		Point 4>>>>>>			Point 5>>	Closing >>	

Figure 3.4 Gantt chart

Remember, there is only so much that we can talk about in our allotted time; and equally there is only so much that our audience can take on board from what we say. So although it may be highly frustrating to have to leave out some of the information that we would like to impart, we have to keep on reminding ourselves what we are there for in the first place. We are *not* there to show off how much we know about our chosen subject area. We *are* there to impart knowledge, ideas or original thought to our listeners. Remember that and we won't go far wrong!

Summary

- Start considering the content of a presentation at the earliest opportunity in order to give maximum thinking time.
- Don't take everything you find on the internet at face value.
- Sort the necessary information from the inconsequential by using a technique such as spider diagrams.
- For formal presentations, consider using the 'Tell 'em times three' formula.
- The structure of a presentation is all-important.
- Think of a suitable way to grab the audience's attention right at the start of a presentation.
- Most people can only remember three or four key points from a presentation.
- Consider the use of visuals when presenting numerical data.

INSTANT TIP

Identify key messages and use a logical structure to create a central theme.

04

How can I make best use of scripts and notes?

It doesn't matter how well we have prepared for our presentation if, when it comes to giving it, we foul up on its delivery. Some people are natural performers, but the truth is that many of us lose confidence when it comes to standing up in front of others and talking from the heart.

It is an unfortunate fact that something that most people tend to take for granted so often ends up as a confused set of ideas. If you asked two normally sane people individually about their ability to communicate together they would probably see no problems on their side; yet when disaster strikes it is invariably found that they have not understood one another's viewpoints.

But communication has to encompass all parties in the process and to take into account all the implications, otherwise by its very nature it has failed. Yet it is often found that communication channels are invariably built in a haphazard way and tend to fall off, the higher up in the organisation you go.

Chief executives and senior management are notoriously bad in the way they communicate their thoughts and ideas to the rest of the organisation. If something is obvious to them, then why can't the workforce see it too? Similarly, just because an organisation 'knows' its products and services are superior to those of its competitors, why can't every idiot on the High Street see that too?

The answer is simple. Each of us is bombarded by information every minute of our lives; so much so that we all take it for granted. Yet we base our decisions to do anything on our experiences, knowledge and feelings – often brought on by a feel-good factor which is continually changing. The busy director may not even realise that his knowledge base could be totally different from that of one of his subordinates and he therefore may neglect to pass on what he regards as perfectly obvious, whereas others might not have that knowledge with which to have come to that conclusion in the first place. And if the company staff are being kept in the dark, what possible hope is there for the customers or suppliers to read the minds of the company directors?

It is not just assumptions that have to be addressed, but the delivery too. Few speakers have the knack of holding the attention of an audience for over half an hour without any notes whatsoever. Those that do can make a stunning impression as being both authoritative and displaying charisma only dreamed of by others. No; they are in the minority. The majority of us need some kind of visual support to keep us going.

Speakers' notes can be a lifeline for many, and they can be used in a variety of different ways to minimise nerves, and to keep our minds focused on what it is we wish to impart to our audience.

How we prepare our notes and how we then get to use them can, however, make an indelible impression on the delegates and be one of the main reasons that our presentation will succeed or fail.

Preparing word for word: not necessarily the best policy

There are some who use their visual aids – which we will come to in the next chapter – as reminders of what it is they want to say. Done well, it can be highly effective. But this can also be a dangerous practice. Who hasn't sat through at least one presentation where it appears that the speaker is literally reading straight off the projected slides? This approach is doomed to failure as the speaker is immediately perceived as someone who does not know his own material and whose delivery is boring, to put it mildly!

Some speakers write out their speeches word for word. And then they read it out word for word and the end result can be pretty dire. I say 'can' as there are some situations where this approach is well warranted. For instance, if what we say is going to be 'on the record' then it may be essential to have every word carefully crafted into a final presentation. Politicians, for instance, have learned that whatever they say has a habit of coming back to haunt them maybe years later; so they are usually very careful about getting the exact phrase or wording thought out well in advance. As often as not they will use the services of a professional speech writer to craft the speech for them; but most presentations are prepared by the people who will give them.

When writing a script that is going to be read verbatim, there are a few dos and don'ts that should always be followed. The fact is that in real life we never speak the way 'good' English is presented on a page. We tend to use incomplete sentences; we use *I'm* and *we'll* and *you're*, rather than *I am*, and *we will* and *you are*. And we tend to use shorter words and phrases rather than pompous rambling sentences. So when writing a speech it is important to follow this style. If we compare the English of someone talking on the radio, for instance, it is very different to that which we will read in a newspaper.

Some words which work well in written English are not normally found in the spoken language. You might *write* 'utilise' but you would *say* 'use'. You might 'comment' on something on paper, but 'say' something when spoken. The lesson here is to avoid the formal use of English which sounds unnatural when read out aloud.

Few people are able to read a script that sounds natural – and that is assuming they have written a vocal script that sounds natural rather than a speech written for the eye. Not just that, but a full verbatim script is inflexible. It gives us no chance to pick up on reactions from the audience, or little leeway with which to lead the audience on with rhetorical questions, while it is also all too easy to lose our place in the script when reading.

Perhaps the biggest drawback is the fact that it is very difficult to maintain good contact with our audience while we are reading. And, as we shall see later, good contact is essential to keep them rapt in whatever we have to say. As well as that, as we have to look down towards the script so often, our voice will not project well and this will add to the danger of a bad delivery.

The downside is that for some people it requires courage to dispense with their carefully prepared notes and they try to hold on to anything that might possibly be regarded as being useful in helping them get through their delivery.

One positive aspect of writing out a full script in advance, though, is that we can then read it out loud at rehearsal and have a good idea of how long it will take to deliver. I say 'have a good idea' rather than 'know' as we shall see later that at the event itself there are a number of factors that could alter the overall length.

The main thing about writing out the script in its entirety is that we should not try to memorise it and, ideally, we should not try to read it out at the performance. Instead it should be condensed into speaker's notes, which we will look at in a moment.

Having said that, the time we have spent in preparing our presentation will already have fixed many of the ideas into our memory and all that will then be required is the occasional memory jogger or prompt to help us recall exactly what it is we wish to say.

Autocue

Whenever we watch a TV news bulletin or a staged political rally, or even a TV game show, the chances are that we will see the presenter seemingly tell us the entire story, hardly ever looking at his script. Look a little more closely, however, and we can see his eyes darting backwards and forwards reading from an 'autocue' – simply a piece of glass angled at 45 degrees in front of the TV camera, or in front of the lectern under which a TV monitor has been so positioned that the presenter can see its reflection.

Reading from an autocue might seem to be the ideal solution. Whereas it used to be expensive, there are nowadays computer programs – some of which can be downloaded free off the internet – that will emulate an autocue for us.

But even if we get to use a 'real' autocue, it is not nearly as easy to use as it looks. The idea is for the audience to believe that we are talking to them, rather than reading from the prompt. Of course, by looking straight through the glass screen and focusing our attention on particular members of the audience – just as the TV presenter looks through the screen and straight into the camera lens to make eye contact with the viewers at home – we can have the best of both worlds. In other words we can keep eye contact with the audience and be able to read from our prepared speech at the same time. What we must not forget, however, is that when we focus on a member of the audience, we lose focus on the script and vice versa. But certainly with practice this can be overcome and an autocue facility can prove to be a boon, especially for people who must give many different presentations and who have the luxury of being able to do so in a more formal setting.

Having someone write our speech for us

Busy executives and politicians will often be able to use the services of a professional speech writer, as we have already noted, although this option is not usually available for lower and middle managers, except perhaps for important occasions in the organisation's calendar of events. But such a speech will still come across as far more convincing if it is converted into good notes from which it can be reassembled 'on the fly'. The fact is that many speeches by public figures are unimpressive simply because they think they can get away with ignoring this fundamental rule.

I have written many speeches for CEOs and public figures and what I find works the best is that, instead of them telling me what they think they want to say, I actually interview them – a little like a journalist firing questions at them from all different angles and perspectives. Of course, I first try to ascertain the key points that they wish to put across. But after that initial stage, by asking them questions, they invariably find that it takes them down avenues that they might not otherwise have thought about; or more importantly it makes them stop and think whether they are using terminology that the audience might not understand, or whether they are assuming the audience knows things they do not, and so on.

I will then go away and write the speech and get them to read it through for meaning, context and overall length. Once they are happy with the content, I then take it away again and reduce the speech down into a series of bullet points. Each bullet should by its nature have enough information to remind the speakers what it is they are saying at this point in time, but they should not be written out as an entire phrase. They, the speakers, must use their brain power to convert those bullets back into something that sounds as if they are speaking from the heart.

Notes are certainly the best option when we have detailed knowledge of the subject on which we are presenting. They also, by their very nature, force us to use a conversational style of delivery, rather than being more formal; and this by its nature is easier on our audience.

The downsides are that we need to remember more of the detail rather than having it spelt out in front of us; and off-the-cuff remarks can sometimes either be misinterpreted, or go badly wrong – as Gerald Ratner, the CEO of a once-thriving group of jewellery stores, famously found to his cost when presenting to an annual conference of the Institute of Directors. In what was meant to be a humorous aside, he was highly derogatory about a particular item that his stores sold. His quote was picked up by the *Sun* newspaper and splashed across the news stands. The rest, as they say, is history. Ratners the jeweller was forced into bankruptcy.

Cards or sheets?

How we present the speaker's notes is of course an important factor, and not something that has a simple or single answer. Some use full sheets of paper, while others use prompt cards that are smaller, typically 15 x 8cm, and, by definition, contain less information on them.

Cards have the advantage that they are easier to hold and they won't rustle. Perhaps more importantly, they won't amplify any trembling hand movements if our nerves get the better of us, which can happen to even the most seasoned speakers.

Some people prefer to place their cards on a nearby table, allowing them to glance down for a prompt when needed. When a card is finished with, it should simply be slid out of the way, rather than turned over, as this otherwise draws unnecessary attention to it.

Paper, on the other hand, can be printed out neatly from a word processor; and if we have a lectern or a side table on which we can place those pieces of paper, then this is often a better option.

I normally recommend my speakers to use a print size of around 16 points. Even if we have excellent eyesight, we never know until the event itself whether the lighting is going to be good or just adequate, and that extra-large size can make all the difference, especially if we want to add dramatic impact by moving away from our one chosen spot. Each page should end at a natural break, not in the middle of a paragraph, as this allows the speaker to have a slight pause without it being obvious to the listener.

Upper-case nightmare

Another thing to be avoided at all costs – contrary to popular belief – is using all upper-case (capital) letters. It actually makes it *harder* to read the script, not easier. And it also leads to problems, as a TV news anchor on a particular Middle Eastern satellite TV station found to his cost on numerous occasions when he delivered unrehearsed stories talking about 'us' rather than U.S. (i.e. American, such as *the us army*) – often with highly comical results. (On the other hand, it must surely have increased viewing figures to this station to discover the many ways he could murder the English language on such a regular basis!)

Working the cards

If we go for cue cards, rather than printed out sheets of paper, then on each card, which should contain no more than one section of the presentation, there should be a header indicating the topic being spoken about, no more than half a dozen main bullets, and perhaps indications of what aids to use and when. (These could be stage directions, or reference to an exhibit, or even voice alerts, which we will cover in Chapter 8.) By using different cards for each main point, the particular topic leaps at us as we move from card to card, and also adds sufficient pauses to help us in our delivery.

If we do add stage directions, however, make them look different – a different font, perhaps, or the use of italic, or highlighted in yellow or whatever – otherwise we might end up sounding like Snagglepuss, that famous cartoon lion from the 1960s, whose catchphrase was 'exit stage right' as he finished each scene of the cartoon!

Apart from that, we should *never* forget to number the cards. I have lost count of the number of times I have seen a speaker drop the cue cards, perhaps when nerves kick in, and hastily put them back together again only to find that they are out of order – something that can be highly embarrassing if this is only discovered at the time of delivery!

Prompt sheets can follow a similar layout, or else be a highly condensed version of the main presentation. In fact, if using PowerPoint slides, it can be very useful to print out each slide with its associated speaker notes, one slide per page. (We'll cover the use of PowerPoint in Chapter 5.)

Yet again, some presenters choose to have just one A4 sheet with the entire structure of the presentation laid out as key words only – enough to remind them where they are in their narrative, but leaving the speaker to talk 'off the cuff' for the majority of the time, which, as we have already noted, can be a highly effective method of delivery.

A working example

As an example, let us look at part of a presentation to prospective customers being given by the CEO of a widget company celebrating ten years in the business. The Public Relations division started by sitting down with the CEO and discussing in an interview style what it was he wanted to say. They came up with this segment of his speech which they then asked him to approve.

> Ladies and gentlemen, may I thank you all for joining us on this somewhat cold and blustery day.
>
> As you will probably know, XYZ is celebrating its tenth birthday this year and we thought it would be apposite to give you some background on who we are, what we have achieved over the past decade and how we view the future in this highly dynamic and, dare I say, highly competitive industry.
>
> XYZ is Europe's leading widget company. We're headquartered right here in the heart of Europe and, with the seemingly unstoppable demand for widgets growing year on year, we see great opportunities ahead of us – and we are readying now to seize these.
>
> XYZ has always been something of a world leader – and it has always been our vision to strive for the very best – ever since we were launched in May 1998 to deliver the finest widgets that money could buy. Our mantra is quality over price; never will we compromise on quality purely in order to save on costs.
>
> And it's paying off. Today we remain a leader – we have 46 per cent of Europe's widget market and we are setting new monthly records in terms of the amount of widgets manufactured.
>
> Worldwide we are the second biggest producer – and the gap with our most important competitor is closing fast.
>
> Our client portfolio is very wide, but not limited to, Government officials, VIPs, decision makers, the

Business/Corporate community, sporting and show business celebrities, major event organisers, insurance companies, the health care sector and so on.

But at XYZ, we don't take our leading position for granted. We worked long and hard to get where we are today, but we're not resting on our laurels. Our clients can be quite demanding at times – rightly so, since our business proposition is all about providing extremely high quality widgets at the most economical price possible.

And that's part of the reason why we are experiencing such dynamic growth, and why in our current financial year we are on track to meet a 25 per cent growth in revenue.

We have a buoyant, traditional market for top-class widgets, but that outstanding growth is principally down to increasing worldwide demand for our quality products in the UK, mainland Europe and Asia, as well as the Middle East. In the last financial year, for instance, we contracted 32 new blue chip customers. etc. etc.

Having obtained his approval, the PR team then went ahead and started preparing slides to accompany his speech. For this segment, they prepared four slides:

1 Company logo
2 World map with slogan 'Quality over price'
3 List of principal clients

4 The XYZ Promise:
- i We don't take leading position for granted
- ii We don't rest on our laurels
- iii Quality over price

Next, they created 'bullet point' prompt cards that gave enough information to act as a memory jogger for the CEO, but left it for him to speak 'off the cuff' for a more impromptu performance:

(S1: XYZ Logo + name check)
Greeting – cold & blustery day

XYZ 10th birthday
background & what achieved
future – dynamic – highly competitive
industry

(S2: world map & 'Quality over price')
Europe's leading widget company
HQ heart of Europe
unstoppable demand – great opportunities
– ready to seize

Always world leader
vision: very best – since May 1998 to deliver
finest widgets money can buy
Quality over price; never compromise

Paying off. 46% of Europe's widget
market – new monthly records
Worldwide #2

(Slide 3: List of principal clients)
client portfolio very wide

(Slide 4: The XYZ Promise)
Don't take leading position for granted
Worked long and hard – not rest on laurels
Our clients demanding – business
proposition – quality & price

Dynamic growth >>> 25 per cent revenue
growth

buoyant, traditional market
increasing, worldwide demand
last financial year, 32 new blue chips

Note the way in which they have inserted a very brief synopsis of what is on each slide so that the CEO can see at a glance that he is talking in sync with what is being shown on screen.

The CEO can also choose whether to use prompt cards or have a few pieces of A4 paper as his memory jogger since the slide prompts, which the PR people have placed in italics, amply break up the bullet-pointed script.

While he is rehearsing his presentation, the CEO will probably start off reading from his script, but as he gets to know it better he can then change over to the prompt cards, enabling him to put across the same message, but in a much more natural ad lib style.

Summary

- Few speakers have the knack of holding the attention of an audience for over half an hour without any notes whatsoever.
- Keep your notes short and to the point.
- Few people are able to read a script verbatim and make it sound natural.

INSTANT TIP

Creating prompt cards or sheets helps ascertain that the structure of the presentation is correct.

05

How can I add flavour to my presentation to make it more interesting?

Once we have decided what we want to say, it is well worth while considering the use of presentation aids. Even though we may have a wonderful voice, the use of these aids can add many extras to help bring almost any presentation to life.

For a start, they can attract attention. Since the sound of one voice can tire the listener if there are no interruptions, so can it be said that the variety afforded by adding certain aids helps an audience focus their attention and stimulate flagging interest.

That's not to say that presentation aids can replace the presenter. With all the modern technology around, be they video, multimedia, software programs and the like, it is still an undeniable fact that at the end of the day, the very best audio-visual aid is a human being with his or her own arsenal of voice, facial expressions, hand gestures and other mannerisms.

So don't make a point of simply reaching out for a laptop computer and a projector. Many excellent presentations specifically do not use visual aids as there is then nothing to get in the way of the presenter as far as the audience is concerned. Think first whether visual aids will add value to your presentation.

Adding visual interest

Various aids are used to influence people's sensory modes and research has shown over and over again that in presentations where the speaker used audio and visual aids, the listeners retained that message much better.

Just compare listening to a radio news bulletin with watching and listening to a TV news bulletin. Normally one would expect the TV output to impart much more information to the viewer than the radio counterpart ever could. And in some ways this is true. Pictures of a disaster almost always have more impact than simply describing it – as disaster agencies helping with famine and in war zones can testify only too well.

The radio producer, on the other hand, will tell you that because the pictures have all but taken over prime importance in the TV news show, the words are dumbed down to fit with the visual content. The radio presenter's mantra is that the best pictures are in our minds, and that therefore more information, not less, can be imparted to the audience. As always in such situations, there is no right and wrong answer to this!

In general, though, and certainly in the presentation arena, words on their own are not always the best method of imparting information. If a subject is unfamiliar, better comprehension is often achieved if we can see a picture or can reach out and touch that object. A map, for instance, can often help in directing someone to a destination where mere words alone can leave the recipient as lost as he ever was. Statistics are also far easier to comprehend if graphs and histograms are used to illustrate the points being made.

We all know the expression 'a picture paints a thousand words' – and so it does. And the memory is often helped enormously when there is something visual to grasp on to rather than a string of words that the brain has much more difficulty remembering. So let's use such an aid if it will add interest and sparkle to our presentation.

In all cases, without exception, the mantra should always be 'use visual aids only if they assist the understanding of our audience. Do not use them if they are merely there to act as a crutch or a substitute for our notes'.

Getting back to the male vs female debate, it is interesting to note that women often think better in terms of visual parallels, and in 3D, compared to their male counterparts. Many experiments have been carried out showing that men find it easier to visualise directions from a map, while women prefer to be given instructions along the lines of 'turn right at the blue building, go straight up the road until you see a garage on your left and then look out for the entrance just after the For Sale board nailed to the oak tree'.

On the other hand, we should make sure we don't get carried away with our presentation aids to the point where they appear to take over the show. Some are more of a hindrance than anything else and if, for instance, things go wrong – perhaps with the sequence of our slides, or a projector breaking down – we can be pretty sure that the disaster will be the one thing that everyone remembers rather than our message.

Use aids to reinforce

As a general rule of thumb, whatever aids we use should reinforce our message rather than distract from what we are trying to put across. They certainly shouldn't be too complicated and there shouldn't be too many of them, or else there is a danger that they themselves will become the star of the show and trample all over our key messages.

Unfortunately there are some people who use visual aids as a means of distracting the audience from themselves. Appropriate visual aids should only be used if they assist the understanding of the audience. They should certainly not be used if they are there simply to act as a substitute for our own notes. If they are introduced without any real thought behind them, then they can even become distractions to our talk rather than helping us get the message across.

Their use must be well thought out and match the style and content of our presentation and, with skill and practice, they can be used to turn even the most potentially dull presentation into something well worth listening to.

So what general principles apply?

The first and most important point about using aids is that they should bring some kind of advantage to our listeners. So if, for instance, we are showing off an object to illustrate the point we are making, it is really important that everyone should be able to see what we are talking about, rather than just a lucky few right at the front of the audience.

If the aid is unfamiliar, we should also take the time to describe its intricacies and for each exhibit we are showing, rather than rely on the audience to work these out for themselves; for not only may it not be obvious to some, but by using brain power to work it out for themselves, they will, by definition, not be giving us their full attention.

What situations would be helped by visual aids?

Aids can be really useful as markers within our presentation – that is, advertising the main point in the talk by emphasising that particular moment. It is undeniable that when we introduce something visual to back up our spoken words, the retention by the audience of that key point is helped.

Using aids when presenting figures also helps in the impact of the presentation as there are many who find data – particularly figures – hard to visualise; so graphs and bar charts do an excellent job here of guiding the listeners to grasp the fundamentals of what we are trying to say.

And if we have an object that we can hand around the audience, it also gives us an excuse to get close to our listeners – perhaps even walking among them as we talk about the object in question. That may not be appropriate on some occasions, but when it is – when we are able to interact on such an intimate level – it can only help in the way we come across to those who have chosen to come to listen to us.

The not-so-simple flip chart

From flip charts and whiteboards to slides and computer images, there is a huge range of aids to choose from, all of which can help in getting our message across. For small audiences – maybe up to, say, 20 – flip charts and whiteboards can be useful for writing straight onto when getting the audience to participate in the discussion, and as such they are an essential part of training presentations where getting audience feedback is often a crucial element in the success of a training course.

Remember, though, that as the flip chart is being prepared 'live', its final appearance needs to have been thought about in advance, or there is a danger it could end up as meaningless jumbles of words, which help nobody.

So if, for instance, you were listing the pros and cons of a particular argument, you could simply divide the chart into two and place the pros on one side and the cons on the other. You could even use different coloured pens to emphasise these points further: green for pro and red for con, for instance, with explanations in blue and titles in black.

Remember, too, that the size of the writing is most important. More than four or five words to a line might render the chart illegible to delegates at the back of the room; some presenters ask for a volunteer to do the writing while they are doing the talking as this helps them to keep eye contact with the audience and the presentation doesn't slow down in order to get the words onto the chart.

Making a point of thanking the delegates for their thoughts as these are written down on the chart is also useful in making them feel more involved in the presentation, which at this point can even verge on a two-way discussion, as long as we are always in control of the direction such two-way discussions can lead. If we do use the audience for such feedback, we should make sure we refer on at least one occasion to the points given in order to demonstrate that there was some point in eliciting their feedback in the first place and that it was not simply used to fill time!

When working with a flip chart, we must be careful where we stand. This might seem obvious, but many presenters fall into this very easy trap. For effective presentation, we should stand to the side of the chart, and angle it in such a way that we can still be seen to be talking to our audience and not to the chart itself!

If we have to point to anything on the chart, it is best if we use a laser pointer, or something else such as a ruler or even a pen, rather than using our hand which always leaves us with the danger of blocking someone's view. I often use an extendable pointer which started life as a fold-away aerial on a transistor radio!

Look at any TV station and the way that the weather presenter uses the map as a visual aid, and still manages to talk to her audience despite pointing out the areas of interest on the map. The map adds focus to what is being said, but it does not replace what is being said. The weather presenter still concentrates her attention on the home audience, and the maps almost appear and disappear without any pre-conceived thought on her part. (The fact that this is all strictly timed and rehearsed should not be apparent to the viewer if the TV technicians and presenter are doing their job well.)

Though flip charts have largely been overtaken by electronic media, they still have a very useful function in presentations – especially training presentations where the use of a flip chart can make a welcome break from staring at endless projected slides as well as giving a personal touch, especially when the presenter takes 'time out' to create pages in her own handwriting.

And one final use, which should never be forgotten … We never know when there will be a power cut or a computer failure just waiting to stymie our presentation. Remember Murphy's Law: if anything can rear its ugly head to make problems for us, you can guarantee it will happen when we are live in front of an audience! So a flip chart can also be a lifesaver in such a situation.

Projected slides and images

Although 35mm slides and overhead projected acetates are still used, they are definitely on their way out, having given way to the ubiquitous PC. Now that computer projectors are falling in price and their quality is improving all the time, most people will immediately think of using their computer when choosing their visual aids.

Video in the form of tapes and DVDs can also add interest along the way since they can demonstrate a process or an event in ways that still pictures could never achieve; and if used properly they can add a highly professional touch to the proceedings. But be careful. If anything is likely to go wrong, you can guarantee that it will be with the use of video; and one thing that throws many people is that video clips saved as files on their computers will very often not show up when projected onto a screen, since the video drivers on their PC motherboards are often incompatible with the video output from which the projector is fed. Do not assume that because you can see a video clip on your computer screen that it will be visible when that screen is projected onto a wall!

Touchy-feely

The use of models or samples can also bring interest to an audience that is starting to flag. I have often used them to good effect, since the actual feeling and texture of something brings any subject to life, while for those who have not yet been able to handle the sample or object, there is a sense of expectancy of what they are about to experience.

In fact the most memorable aids are not only those we can touch, but those which we can smell or taste as well. For instance, when giving presentations to audiences about living and working in Saudi Arabia, I used regularly to throw bottles of oudh perfume into the audience. For a start, the bottles were presented in little velveteen boxes – a really touchy-feely wrapping. I would then 'dare' them to try some, while also telling them that my wife hated me wearing the stuff as she thought the smell was revolting, and that it lingered for hours. How could they possibly resist just a sniff? I would end the presentation by burning oudh incense and together this made the entire presentation one that was talked about for many months afterwards!

Likewise on another occasion I offered up a sample of Mao Tai – an infamous Chinese liqueur made from fermented sorghum that was 'popularised' in the West by President Richard Nixon on his famous visit to Peking in 1972 – to a volunteer from the audience. Some people have described the taste as akin to the smell of the elephant house at London Zoo! Most would agree that the taste has a habit of lingering after it is consumed. Some would argue that it gives new meaning to the old expression, 'First prize a taste of Mao Tai; second prize *two* tastes of Mao Tai!'

Death by PowerPoint

I have deliberately left the most commonly used visual aid to the end of this chapter. Electronic visual aids are by far the most common – and expected – aids and there is hardly anyone who would not first consider the use of the most popular software package in this arena: namely Microsoft's PowerPoint. (There are, of course, plenty of other presentational software programs around, including the free office suite, OpenOffice, which can be downloaded from www.openoffice.org, and which is certainly PowerPoint's equal.)

How many of us have sat through PowerPoint presentations that have almost sent us off to sleep, made little sense and at the very least have made us cringe. The 'Death by PowerPoint' syndrome is something that most people who have sat through such presentations can readily identify with.

Yet, if you think about it, PowerPoint is amazing. Who among us wouldn't have given our eye teeth for such a software program two or three decades ago when the best we could hope to come up with were 35mm slides that often needed to be prepared weeks in advance of the event? So why should such an amazing visual aid be so fraught with danger?

Well, there are as many dos and don'ts to do with PowerPoint as there are pointers for good presentations. So let's look at some of the things people get up to with this software, and see how we can use it to add value to our presentation, rather than to kill it stone dead.

Just as with the speech itself, PowerPoint slides need shaping and a structure that complements the speech.

They are NOT a one-size-fits-all proposition. The fact that so many people use their slides for display, whilst also giving them out as handouts and even using them as prompts, as they try desperately to steer a middle path hoping that they will serve all three purposes, means they run the risk that they end up not achieving any of those three targets. We should only use the slides to add value to our presentation. If we want to give out handouts, we can adapt the slides for that specific purpose; and if it is useful, we can even add our own prompt notes by going to Notes Page in the View menu and printing out a set of notes pages solely for our use. As an absolute minimum, the slides should have the following sections:

- Title – as the name suggests this slide will tell our audience what to expect of us. We can add the objective of the presentation as well so that our audience understands the general direction of our talk.
- Table of contents – again this allows our audience to know what they can expect from us, and amplifies the journey on which we are going to take them. Many would argue that a table of contents is not strictly necessary, given the title slide before this. As always in cases like this it depends on the circumstances. The main thing, though, is that we shouldn't add too many points here, or there could be a danger that our audience will make up their minds before we have even started that we are going to be long and boring!
- Main section – we'll come to the layout in a moment.

- Conclusions – every presentation should have a conclusion, which we hope our audience will take on board and think about when they are making their way home. So we should have a slide outlining the most important points we want our audience to take away from the presentation: the 'tell them what we have told them' point from our *tell 'em* trilogy that I described earlier. Remember that they will have taken in a lot of information and they simply won't be able to retain all of it that easily. Anything we can do to help in this direction has to be a good thing, surely?
- Questions – most presentations benefit from a 'Q&A' session at the end. A simple slide saying 'Questions', or perhaps simply a '?' may be all that is needed here.

How difficult can it really be to design something as simple as a slide?

It is often said that the most difficult things in life are also the most simple. Perhaps nowhere is this more true than in designing slides for a presentation. Here the golden rule – KISS – applies:

Keep It Simple Stupid!

Many will argue over how many slides one should actually use in a presentation. I have actually seen it argued that one slide for every six minutes of talking is ample, though

I have to say that I would disagree on that point. As always … it depends!

But what this does lead on to is what is often referred to as the 6-6-6 rule:

We should have no more than:

- 6 points per slide
- 6 words per point
- 6 text slides in a row.

(If you were in agreement with the one-slide-every-six-minutes rule, then I guess this would be the 6-6-6-6 rule!)

In other words, we should NEVER cover more than six different points on one slide; NEVER have more than six words describing the point we are trying to make; and NEVER have more than six text slides in a row without breaking up the sequence by having some kind of graphic or picture slide to avoid it getting visually boring.

Putting too much information on one slide has two important drawbacks: firstly it makes the slide look far too cluttered and people at the back of the room may have great difficulty reading it; for a slide to have impact, it should be kept short and sweet!

Secondly, if the slide contains everything we wish to tell our audience, then why should they bother listening to us in the first place? They could simply read the slide and switch off to our voice – which is what invariably happens in such a scenario. Worse still, they may flip ahead to a point we are not even talking about and get totally out of sequence in the argument we are trying to put across. Remember: if your visual aids say as much or even more than the presenter does, then one of them is unnecessary!

This dual scenario is often what lies behind the so-called Death by PowerPoint syndrome. But it can also be caused by bad design of the slides themselves.

Packages such as PowerPoint and OpenOffice offer template slides that we can use as the basis for our slide show; but not all of them are suitable for giving presentations and we should think long and hard about just what it is we are trying to put across.

Some would even argue that few of the pre-packaged templates are actually any good and that those that are reasonable have been seen by most audiences at some time or another on many occasions. You might, therefore, consider designing your own unique template and saving it as a '.pot' file, or even purchasing professionally designed templates online. (A quick Google search should list many designer templates for download and purchase.)

Any commercial designer will tell us that individual colours are associated with emotions. Black may be classy or add a touch of glamour in some scenarios, but it also has negative connotations such as mourning. Red can look striking, but there is a danger of it being too 'in-your-face'. Green can be soothing, but too vibrant a green can have the opposite effect. Purple has a royal or ethereal feel to it; but make it slightly lighter so it verges on pink and there is a whole new feel about it; and so on.

Cool colours work best for backgrounds as they tend to recede away from us. Warm colours work best in the foreground which is why one of the most common PowerPoint colour schemes is yellow text on a blue background. If you will be giving your presentation in a darkened room, then a light coloured text on a dark background works well. If, however, you intend to give your presentation in a lightened room, then a light background with dark text works better.

Whole treatises have been written on the power of colours, and it is not for nothing that multinational corporations have been known to pay thousands of pounds to design agencies to come up with the perfect combination of the right colours on their corporate logos.

The main thing to remember as always is that the background of the slide should enhance our presentation, not get in the way of it. As a rough rule of thumb, we are generally safe in our business presentations if we stick to a white, grey, yellow or light blue background.

Unfortunately, not all projectors can project true colour onto the screen, particularly backgrounds. This is especially true of cheaper or older models of projector, or if the light bulb inside is getting old.

Of course, colours that are dull or blend in with the text in any way should be avoided. And if the background is too bright it can make the font appear fuzzy, making it difficult to read. Having a picture behind the text can also allow that text to get lost in the background.

In general, serifed fonts should be avoided; sans-serif is far easier to read under difficult lighting conditions. The more 'curly-wurly' the font, the more difficult it will be to read. Arial, Tahoma or Verdana, for instance, are easy to read; Times, Garamond and Georgia are more difficult; highly serifed such as *Lucida Calligraphy*, *Brush Script* or *Monotype Corsiva*, are very difficult.

Likewise we should not use upper-case (capital) letters throughout, as again they are much more difficult to read, and in this internet age, UPPER-CASE LETTERS ARE ASSOCIATED WITH SHOUTING!

As a general rule of thumb, title words should be anywhere between 36 and 44 points in size; primary matter should lie in the range 28–32 points; and secondary matter should be between 24 and 28 points high. Smaller font sizes render the slide unreadable so, again, we should avoid this at all costs. So:

Title words
Primary matter
Secondary matter

And another rule – the 2-2 rule – tells us:

- No more than 2 font types per slide.
- No more than 2 font colours in a slide.

Yet again, simplicity is the name of the game. We mustn't let our fun in creating amazingly psychedelic and busy slides get in the way of the message. In general, we should always follow the slogan: If in doubt, leave it out!

So again, under this formula, we should use animations sparingly. True, they can help focus the audience on what we want them to focus on and they can also help reduce the clutter on the slide as individual points can be made to appear one by one. But the downside of this is that we may be so busy timing our speech to the bullet points as they fly in from the margins, or so wrapped up pressing the *next* sequence as we make our points, that the whole effect comes across as contrived.

A very simple rule with regards to the use of clip art is avoid it at all costs! In the 'good old days' when PCs were not as ubiquitous as they are today, clip art looked cool and classy. But while it might have looked great in its day, that day is now long past!

If you want to use graphics, then a good quality photograph which you can take with a digital camera or download off the internet (but beware of copyright violations!) can be used. If the image is secondary to the point being made, it can sometimes help to soften the edges by adding Gaussian blur or using the motion filter in Photoshop or some similar software package; if the image is important to what is being said, then try to restrict the amount of text being used or even have no text at all on that slide.

And finally: Be very careful with spellings. People just love reading other people's spelling and grammatical mistakes. Somehow it can make us all feel superior to spot other people's mistakes. Long after the show is over, it is those errors that will be remembered! So *it I very impotent to cheque you're speling. You do not wont to hav yor audiens theenk you were bad in yor skool – even if you was.*

Summary

- Whatever aids we use should reinforce our message rather than distract from what we are trying to put across.
- The most memorable aids are those that can be smelt, felt or tasted.

INSTANT TIP

When dealing with PowerPoint, follow the basic rule of KISS – Keep it Simple Stupid!

06

How can I best prepare for the presentation?

However good we may think we are, there is never any substitute for a good rehearsal prior to our performance. Not only will a rehearsal help us to judge the timing of the overall speech, it may also help us refine its content, and means we should end up giving a better delivery. And because these reasons mean there is less to worry about come the big day, it should also help to reduce our nerves.

If it is at all possible, a rehearsal in the actual room where the presentation is to be given will be particularly helpful, though very often this is not an option. If it is possible, however, it means we can judge the lighting and make adjustments as necessary; the height of the podium or table, if provided, can also be adjusted, for a surface that is too high or too low for our notes can be worse than useless.

If we intend to use visual aids, it means we can also judge what works well and what works badly; and if that means we get to try out the controls of any peripheral equipment we are likely to use, then again this has to be a good thing. It is one of those ridiculous facts that it always seems to be the small, seemingly inconsequential things that have a habit of tripping people up, rather than the bigger items that people concentrate their efforts upon.

Two-headed presentations need particular preparation

Presentations that involve two or more speakers have a particular record of tripping up the unwary and such performances need even more rehearsal than any other. It is no use assuming that our co-presenter understands what we take for granted. Going through who is responsible for saying what, how each will hand over to the other, how any aids used will actually be introduced and by whom, how the Q&A session at the end will be handled, and so on, will greatly reduce the likelihood of accidents.

I remember on one occasion doing a double header with someone who would insist on throwing in ad libs on every conceivable occasion. Not only did this disrupt the flow of the overall theme, which caused concentration difficulties for the audience, but by 'thinking on her feet' instead of sticking to our rehearsed presentation, she actually ruined the punch line or climax of a number of points to which we were building up, and so all but ruined what could have been a very impressive performance.

How should I rehearse?

It's a fact that many people feel highly self-conscious when talking to an empty room. They convince themselves that it really is all right to skip over bits of the presentation on the basis that they 'know' that bit. Similarly they may mumble their way through their speech, assured that they will be able to enunciate clearly on the big day.

If a rehearsal is worth doing at all – and it is – then it is worth doing it properly.

Invariably it is the first two or three minutes – the overall opening – that should be rehearsed the most. First impressions count for everything when we are giving a speech or presentation. If the audience has had enough of us before we have even got into our stride then we will have lost them for ever and we might just as well give up at this point.

The corollary of this is that if we can feel that they are already on our side, then this will act to boost our level of confidence, resulting in a better performance, which will further boost the audience's appreciation of our performance: a classic positive feedback loop as would be described by physicists.

Timing should of course always be checked as we read through our speech; but we must remember that this can only ever be approximate, especially if we are talking from notes and therefore creating a unique speech every time we go through it. Because of audience feedback, different acoustics and a number of other things that can occur during a live performance, we should remember that the actual presentation will typically last around 20 per cent *longer* than our rehearsal would suggest. Yet many people speak faster in front of an audience than they would when they are relaxed and the adrenalin hasn't kicked in; but again, to counter that, when we react to the way in which we perceive the audience and how we make eye contact with them, it tends to slow proceedings down a little. So what happens in reality is that the overall length is similar to the rehearsal timings, but we find we are talking faster while pausing longer. By all means make longer pauses – this is an excellent way of adding gravitas or drama to an argument, but we should be very careful about speaking faster as this can make it difficult for some people to understand and capture every word.

On my training courses I suggest to those who have a propensity to speak fast to colour in some 'traffic lights' – small red, yellow and green highlighter dots – in key positions on their notes. I tell them to imagine that every time they see one of these traffic lights coming up to slow down and be ready to pause (since this is a road junction!) and then to accelerate slowly into their next piece of verbiage. The change of pace and the deliberate pauses make the delivery much more exciting and noteworthy, and the fact that they are thinking about their delivery, albeit somewhat subconsciously, helps them with their speed.

Of course, it is also possible that we over-rehearse; that we are so word perfect that come the actual event we have lost any sense of spontaneity. The trick is knowing when to stop! Equally if we have very little time in which to prepare, then it may be a good idea simply to rehearse the 'difficult' bits, such as the start and the end and any key sections in between.

Rehearsing in front of a hand-picked audience can be extremely advantageous, not least because they may see areas that need attention, or that don't follow through very well. They can also advise on whether the speed of delivery is right, whether jokes work well or fall flat, and so on.

Ideally there should be two or three people only in our rehearsal audience. They can be work colleagues, friends or even family – just so long as they are prepared to be both objective about what we are doing and to give honest feedback. Simply to be told that we are wonderful does us no favours in the long term! We should recall that famous movie one-liner: *love is never having to say you're sorry*. Good friends and work colleagues will hopefully tell us what we need to be told, rather than what we want to be told!

Sometimes this might require us to be thick skinned. I remember my early attempts at giving speeches and presentations when my wife would act as my rehearsal audience. She would give me loads of feedback – much more than I was comfortable with, if the truth be known. Why couldn't she see my point of view? What did she mean I was speaking too fast? Couldn't she see that I was giving dramatic impact at that point? Why couldn't she see the logic of the statements I was giving out?

But she was right. She could see things that I never could, and once I got over the initial upset, and realised she was only trying to help, things became very much easier to correct. Remember, too, that women tend to think and follow arguments in different ways from men. For a start, as we have already noted, they are much more able to think laterally, but also tend to pictorialise situations in their brains more than men do. So if you are a man, make sure there is a woman in your rehearsal audience, and vice versa.

Criticism should be welcomed – but only if it is helpful and gives clear areas for improvement. If all we get are comments such as 'that's dreadful', then it's time to change our hand-picked audience because all this will do is to sap our confidence. But constructive criticism should be warmly welcomed. If our hand-picked audience won't tell us the truth then the only way we can ever find out if things need changing is when it is all too late.

If we are unable to get a rehearsal audience together, then a second best scenario is to use a video recorder to get feedback on our performance. The camera should be positioned about halfway back in the hall or room so as to give us a picture of how we will come across to those who are not sitting right at the front. This will give useful pointers about our positioning, the way we use visual aids, the speed of our delivery and how well we project our voice, not to mention our use of body language (see Chapter 8).

How do I control my nerves?

All performers, be they musicians, actors or presenters, get attacks of nerves. It happens to the most practised of professionals and not just to novices. For some, the hand trembling syndrome is all too prevalent; others feel weak in the knees; many get sweaty palms while others find they start to stammer or get tongue tied. There are those who feel the need to rush to the bathroom increasingly frequently, especially just before they go on stage; and of course many are in such a state of panic they practically forget everything! Learning how to deal with nerves or stage fright – call it what we will – is what can make or break a performance of whatever category.

In reality, an attack of nerves is actually no bad thing. It is one way that the body gets the adrenalin flowing, keying us up to give our best performance. In fact, if we didn't feel nervous about a performance, it could end up lacklustre. So let us welcome our nervous energy and learn how to control it!

For a start, however nervous we feel, the chances are that our audience will hardly notice, if at all. What might give us away is a trembling hand – amplified by holding a sheaf of loose papers – or parched lips.

Yet, if we consider what it is that makes us nervous, the chances are that it comes down to a number of irrational fears. We may feel we cannot rise to the expectations of the audience. We're afraid of drying up in front of them; of not being able to put two words together coherently; of making a fool of ourselves.

So the first thing we should do is to remember why it is we are there in the first place. We were (possibly) invited by people who believed we had something worthwhile to say and they were convinced that we could do it.

We will also have researched our audience, so that we know their make up and what they are likely to know and what they are unlikely to know. We will have rehearsed well, too, and that by itself can act as a safety net so that we are prepared for the unexpected.

Being afraid of making a fool of oneself is probably one of the hardest fears to quell; as often as not we may end up with a dry mouth, and it doesn't seem to matter how many sips of water we take, that parched lip syndrome just seems to keep coming back.

How we handle such panic attacks – and a panic attack is exactly what this amounts to – is the key to getting through this. As Lawrence of Arabia said in that famous film bio, 'The trick is not minding that it hurts'. If we remain calm, we are halfway to conquering it. If we can add some humour to the proceedings, it can even form a common bond with our audience, since we are all only human, and the audience is positively willing us to succeed.

In my early days of public speaking I used to find the dry mouth syndrome particularly debilitating, until one day I was shown a way of getting round it. Picture yourself with someone biting into a soft juicy grapefruit or a lemon.

Stop! What is the first thing that happened just then? Did your mouth water? Because that is often what instinctively happens when someone conjures up such an image. Could we do that to order? Yes of course we could! So perhaps we could picture ourselves talking not to an audience of people, but to an audience of juicy lemons! (Hey – if it works, don't knock it!) But if it somehow doesn't work, it is time to move on to 'plan B' …

Remember we just spoke about injecting some humour into the proceedings? We desperately want to lick our lips and the more we try to hide it from the audience, the worse it gets. So don't try! Embrace it! Tell the audience that as you came in to the room you saw a waiter walking past with a lovely big bowl of fruit piled high with grapefruits and oranges. Paint the picture – and you can guarantee that your audience will start salivating right there in front of you – and the chances are you will too. But even if you don't, the humour will have broken the panic, you will calm down, the audience will be totally on side and potential tragedy will have been turned to success.

Another form of drying up is when the brain, rather than the saliva glands appears to stop working. Somehow we just can't find the word that is on the tip of our tongue; or we forget an important name – one that we use every day. We lose our place in the argument; everything turns blank for a moment and we can't even imagine why we are there, let alone what message we were trying to put across.

Once again, humour can come to the rescue. If we can't find the right word, then highlight the fact that our brain has gone a total blank. Describe it as a senior moment. Everyone has them, and our audience will see us as fallible like everyone else on this planet. And the chances are that the resultant release of tension will soon have those words flowing again nicely.

With some people, their nervous energy finds release in ways that can really annoy their audience, without them even realising it. I'm sure most of us have seen presenters endlessly playing with a ring or pen, stepping backwards and forwards, gripping tightly onto their lectern as if the entire edifice is about to collapse, or using fillers such as 'erm', or 'ya-know-what-I-mean' or 'kind-of-thing'. If such tell-tale signs are obvious, it can highlight to our audience that we are not confident, which in turn can suggest to them that, if we are not confident in what we are presenting, then maybe they should have doubts about what we are saying too.

Yet again, some people are fine when it comes to standing up in front of a few work colleagues; but if there are large numbers in a public audience they tend to dry up. This is a syndrome I used regularly to experience when teaching BBC announcers how to control their nerves in front of the microphone. The thought of some four million people or more out there in the big wide yonder hanging on to their every word was something many found hard to deal with.

With the radio announcers, the remedy was simple. I got them to bring to work a photograph of their girlfriend/boyfriend/spouse/parent, etc., and to place it right beside the microphone and to talk to their special friend, rather than anyone else 'out there'. Not only did this make it a one-on-one experience for them, but the resultant voice that was broadcast sounded warmer and more trusting than had originally come across.

The remedy for TV announcers and news readers is exactly the same as for people giving speeches and presentations. Picture that special friend behind the TV camera – or, in the case of a theatre presentation, picture three friends sitting in the audience – one on either side and one in the middle. Speak to these three; but speak to each of them. That way the audience will feel as if we are speaking to all of them, and we can avoid even having to look them in the eye if indeed that is what is making us nervous.

But can I pre-prepare for a nervous attack?

There are as many nerve-reducing techniques as there are public speakers, not every one of which works for everybody; but possibly one of the following might help:

- Learn to relax – those who practise yoga or deep-breathing exercises or some of the many other relaxation forms often find that these can banish a severe attack of nerves. The old counting-up-to-ten trick while breathing slowly and deeply is used by many presentation 'professionals'.
- Try the technique beloved by those who have to sit in the dentist's chair – tightly gripping a hard or sharp object such as a bunch of keys, the objective being that the slight pain of doing so refocuses their anxieties away from what they were anxious about in the first place.
- Conjure up whatever your definition of success is. Many athletes find that concentrating all their thoughts on winning the race or jumping the furthest, or whatever, can help them actually achieve what they have dreamed about.
- Picture the audience in a ridiculous scenario, such as sitting there in front of you stark naked. Reducing their image into something that puts you into a superior position will enhance your own self-worth at their expense.

But whatever we do, we must not go for a nip of 'Dutch courage'. Although a quick shot of alcohol might make us feel a little better, the chances are that we will perform very much worse. It's a bit like driving. 'Don't drink and drive' has an exact parallel with 'Don't drink and give presentations'. So if we are performing at the end of a meal, that unfortunately means we should avoid having a glass of wine with the meal. Ask the waiter to keep a glass back, if absolutely necessary. But never even think of giving way to temptation to have just a 'little' sip!

And finally, keep preparing to the very last minute

Although we have asked all the necessary and most fundamental questions about the audience and the venue and why we are there and what they are expecting of us, there is really no substitute for meeting the delegates who have actually turned up to hear us.

Now, it may be that there has been a last minute switch of people in the audience; or we may have actually got it wrong as far as our understanding of what they are there for. But if we turn up early we may get a chance to talk to the actual delegates themselves; or if the presentation is 'in-house' where some of the managers might not turn up themselves until the last moment, even shaking a few hands will give us the opportunity to gauge the mood of our listeners. As always, such preparation is never wasted.

Summary

- There is never any substitute for a good rehearsal prior to the performance.
- The first two or three minutes should be rehearsed the most.
- Welcome constructive criticism.
- Welcome nervous energy but learn how to control it!
- Never drink alcohol before giving a presentation.
- Learn how to relax.
- Make a reconnaissance of the room in which you will present well ahead of the event itself if at all possible.

INSTANT TIP

Rehearse your presentation so that you know intimately its structure rather than its content.

What final preparation do I need to think about before the presentation itself?

Good presentation is not just about preparing a speech and presenting it to the audience with the benefit of some slides or other visual aid. If we want our presentation to be successful and memorable then there is still a lot for us to do in preparing for the actual event.

We have so far prepared what it is we want to say and we have put together our visual aids. We have rehearsed the material, thought through any dramatic moments where we might bring in some extra effects to accentuate a particular point; and, now that we have arrived at the event itself, we have to make sure that everything is set up ready for the 'off'.

At what point does speaking become public speaking?

Speaking is a two-way process. Unless we are delivering a Shakespearean soliloquy, the chances are that someone else will be there to interact with us verbally. By definition, therefore, all speaking is a form of public speaking; the only difference is how large that public will be.

The actual difference, though, depends mainly on two things: how large is our audience, and what is the outcome of our talking in the first place.

The size of the audience is obvious enough. Even if we cannot see how large our audience is – and this is something that can affect the nerves of media presenters to a large extent – simply knowing that there are an awful lot of people out there listening to us can play a dramatic part in the way we deliver our presentation.

Likewise, the importance of the event will have a dramatic impact on how we perform. If we go to a job interview, for instance, there may be just one or two people in our audience, but the circumstances will dictate how we feel and be affected by how we perform.

However large or small our presentation is going to be, we cannot afford to relax just before the event itself. This is the time when we must be most prepared; and that preparation includes the layout of the room, the equipment we are going to use, logistics, lighting, travel arrangements – even what we are going to wear.

Where should we position ourselves?

On many occasions, our public speaking might take place sitting around tables rather than standing at the front of a room before an audience. We might have been asked to give a sales pitch, or be at a job interview. We, as often as not, will not have had the opportunity to see the room before the event itself; but if we are able to, choosing where to sit is a very important part of our preparation process.

Obviously we don't want to sit in front of a bright window or else we will appear to our audience as a silhouette, which means they will not have a chance to see our facial expressions and they will miss out on our body language – and as we will see in the next chapter, this is an essential weapon in our armoury of getting our points across.

If available, a corner location is one of the best as we can then see and be seen easily without having to turn around too much. Making eye contact with everyone is important in being able to establish a rapport with them – something essential if we are trying to sell a product or even ourselves, as in a job interview.

Although such scenarios will involve a small audience, they may often have a lot riding on them. What can best be described as a small scale sales pitch may not allow us the luxury of a slide presentation; but the other side of the coin is that we should know whom we are addressing in much more detail than when there are many people present. This means we should be on much firmer ground when we come to define the objective of this presentation in the early stages.

What all salesmen know intrinsically is the old adage: *sell the benefits, not the products.* And this technique should help us in our preparation, such that we can demonstrate our knowledge of the company's aims and problems allowing us to present our solution to their problems – be it that we are the right candidate for the job, or that our widget is the right solution for the company's aims.

I used to have to pitch for a company in which I worked to sign up new clients. It wasn't a task that I relished. Some people make good salesmen, others do not; and I found myself leaning towards the latter category. And then someone pointed out to me the way that politicians handle difficult interviews. They prepare what they want to say, and somehow, irrespective of the question being asked, they turn their answer round to what they wanted to say in the first place, rather than what the journalist wanted to find out. It's a powerful technique and, combined with selling the benefits, not the products, can turn around even the most daunting presentation.

Control of the environment

What most people immediately bring to mind, though, when the term public speaking is first mentioned, is the large theatre venue where we can use all the resources at our disposal – visual aids, body language, audience control and so on. It is in this environment especially that preparation to the minutest detail is absolutely essential.

If we have control of the room layout, or at least have a say in this, then there are a number of things we should remember. Most importantly, room layout should be heavily influenced by the purpose of the meeting, be it a face-to-face exchange, a committee meeting, a seminar or customer presentation.

Room layouts

There are generally six recognised ways of laying out a room for a presentation. As often as not this may already have been dictated by circumstance or else by the shape of the room.

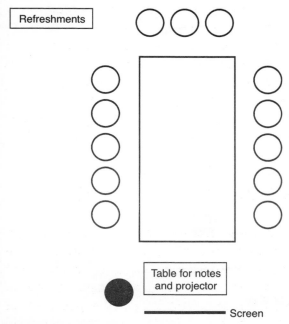

Figure 7.1 Boardroom style

Inside a company, perhaps the most common layout is the boardroom style where everyone sits around a long rectangular or oval table (see Figure 7.1).

Ideal for an audience of around a dozen or so people, the presenter would normally stand at one end slightly off centre in order to give room for the projector and screen (unless the former is mounted on the ceiling) with a little table for notes and other effects slightly off to the side.

Similar in style to a boardroom layout is the circular style in which the long boardroom table is replaced by a large circular table (see Figure 7.2).

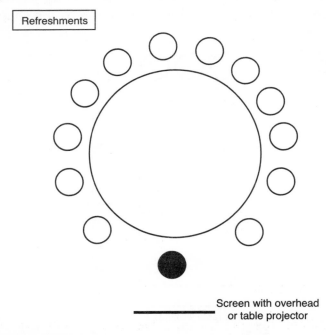

Figure 7.2 Circular style

This type of arrangement encourages open discussion and, with no obvious leader, everyone feels equal to one another.

The horseshoe arrangement is another variant of this which is often found in training sessions, allowing the trainer to walk into the middle of the group and become more intimate with his delegates.

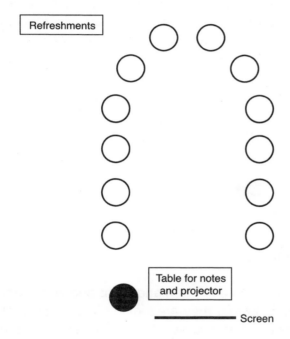

Figure 7.3 Horseshoe style

Sometimes the tables are taken away altogether if a group discussion is likely to take place, but the more formal layout with tables or desks is much better if the delegates are expecting to take notes.

What is known as the cabaret style is often found at formal dinners and with larger audiences.

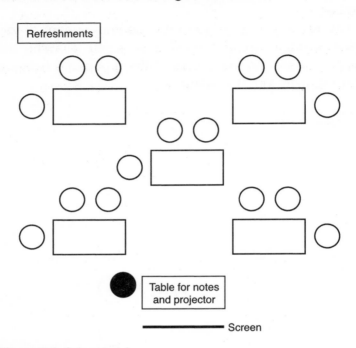

Figure 7.4 Cabaret style

Here we will find between three and eight people at each table, all seated so that they are looking in one direction – at the presenter! If the event is a larger one, it is sometimes set up so that the speaker can stand on a stage or slightly raised area so that everyone is able to see the facial expressions of the presenter, who in turn is also able to see each and every member of the audience. There is a drawback for this kind of seating arrangement in that at formal dinners, you invariably find half the audience having to turn their chairs through up to 180 degrees in order to face the speaker. Although those affected can be somewhat averse to doing do, the up-side of this is that it clearly delineates a break between the informal eating and the more formal presentation.

A classroom style whereby the delegates are seated behind tables laid out in rows, is ideal for seminars.

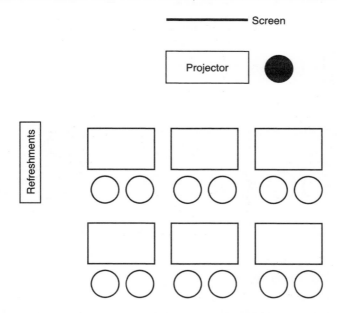

Figure 7.5 Classroom style

It can feel a little like one is back at school, and so for this reason, tables can be placed at angles to one another to give the room more of an organised-haphazard style!

And finally, the theatre style is used for large occasions where those at the back are often higher up than people at the front.

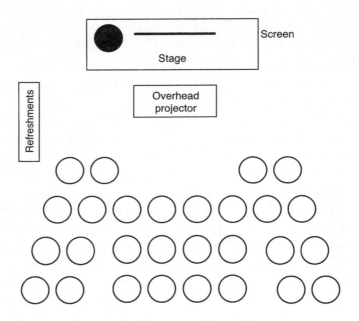

Figure 7.6 Theatre style

A preferred style for news conferences, the speaker or speakers will often deliver their presentation on a stage and their slides might even be projected onto the screen via rear-projection to give a more professional appearance.

Think of the mix

Even if meeting in a small room such as an office, the seat layout can make a dramatic difference to the overall success of that meeting. In one company in which I worked, 'management' met union representatives once a month in a conference room. The managers would file into the room and sit along one side of the long table; and a short while later the union reps would file in and sit opposite them. And what was the result? Not surprisingly every meeting soon broke down into a them-and-us situation. It wasn't aggressive, but the whole consciousness of those present could be defined by whose camp you were sitting in.

Imagine, if you can, how everything changed dramatically a few weeks later when it was decided by the managers to sit randomly around the table, forcing the union reps to sit where there was space available – in other words, among their opposite counterparts. Suddenly conversation wasn't between one party and another, but ended up as everyone searching for a common goal. The meetings were much more productive, and everyone was working for the common good rather than for their own particular piece of territory.

For larger scale meetings, there is usually much more choice in room layout. Firstly, the size of the room should be such that there is plenty of space for everyone present, but not so large that an impression is given that many people couldn't be bothered to turn up!

The quality of the furnishings too can make a difference to the expectations of the audience. If it has a business-like feel to it, then it will help in preparing the audience for a proper business-like meeting; but if there is a degree of tackiness to the décor, it will undoubtedly set the wrong tone.

Environmental concerns such as the right amount of ventilation or air conditioning as well as the level of lighting are essential to consider too. Without adequate ventilation, the amount of body heat generated by the audience could help send them off to sleep during our performance. Remember, it is not for nothing that the majority of commercial airline crews turn up the cabin temperature during night time sectors once they switch off the lights, to ensure that as many people as possible fall asleep.

Lighting needs to be adequate to be able to read our notes, but not too bright if it is going to detract from any projected slides. If the lights are dimmable this is obviously an advantage as we can then better control the ambiance to our own particular purposes.

When considering room layout, the positioning of the slide projector will be paramount, of course. Everyone needs to be able to see those slides without straining to do so. And we will have to position ourselves in such a way that we can also be seen by the audience. Where we have the luxury of choosing where to place the projector, it often works well if the screen is positioned in a corner of a rectangular room, rather than in the centre of a wall.

Wherever we place our equipment, however, be it projector, computer terminal, or even overhead projector, we should always be fastidious about the layout of the power cables. To reduce the risk of mishaps, they should be positioned at the speaker's end of the room and, where possible, any extra length of cable should be coiled up and taped against the leg of a table, for instance. Lengths of cable across the floor should be taped down with 'gaffer's tape'. Not only will this be neater, but there is then less risk of anyone tripping over them, not to mention leaving us wide open to legal action should one of the delegates suffer a mishap from our negligence!

Final checks

It is absolutely essential at this point that we do not rush into anything without making sure that everything is exactly as it should be. In particular any equipment we use should be fully functioning and we should be fully conversant with its controls.

We can't assume that just because the organiser said a particular piece of equipment would be there that it will be there, or even be working properly. So the moment we arrive at the venue our first job is to make sure that everything is where we expect it to be. Although we may have no control over the environment – particularly if we are a guest speaker – we should still ensure we are there in plenty of time to check the room, make any small changes we are able to, and take on board any problem areas that we might not be able to change, but that we can work our way around. Remember that if, for instance, a projector does not work, time must be available for a maintenance engineer to be called and to fix it, rather than be still fiddling with the controls by the time the audience arrives.

We should also check that there is a table or podium, or whatever we have requested for our notes and props, already in position; and if we are assured that 'it will be here in a short while', we should keep on checking that it is on its way, rather than relying on the organiser to keep chasing it. The chances are that the organiser will be very busy just prior to the event, chasing up the 101 other things that can possibly go wrong, and may not put our particular problem at the top of the list of things that must be sorted.

A common problem when plugging a computer into a projection system is that the projector doesn't 'recognise' there is a computer attached. Very often this can be rectified by rebooting the PC so that its video board 'sees' the projector input as it goes through its start up sequence. Some computers even require a 'hard boot' for this to work – in other words completely switching the power of the computer off before switching on again, rather than simply rebooting.

If a microphone system is available, this is also the time to try it out. How many of us have not sat through speeches and presentations where howl-round has occurred because of badly positioned loudspeakers or poorly set up equipment? It is important to remember that the acoustic of a room changes dramatically from the time it is virtually empty to when it is filled with people. Bodies absorb sound, so what might start off as a lively room with lots of echo can become almost dull and lifeless, requiring us to speak up and enunciate better.

We should make sure that the microphone is so positioned that it is in line with our upper lip when we are standing straight. Remember: if we have to adjust the height of the microphone just prior to speaking – perhaps because someone else has been presenting prior to us – we should ensure that the mic is switched off before we adjust it. We should only make adjustments after this, in order that it doesn't make unpleasant jarring sounds that will stay with the audience when we are trying to capture their attention in those crucial opening minutes!

Whatever we do, we should avoid at all costs that awful 'One two; one two; testing testing' that so many speakers feel obliged to utter into the microphone just to ensure it is working!

Clothes maketh the man

Of course, we will also have considered carefully what we are going to wear, since clothes always create an impression and, as we have remarked before, first impressions count! A useful rule of thumb is to 'go one step higher' than our audience. If they are wearing casual clothes such as jeans, we should be wearing smart casual. If the delegates are wearing suits, we should ensure we are wearing our best one. Dark colours tend to give us more authority in this respect.

When I used to perform on the public speaking circuit, as often as not I used to wear one of my vast collection of waistcoats. It was a kind of trademark – something that everyone remembered me by, which was useful if one wanted to be instantly recognised and get more speech bookings! One day I was giving a double-headed presentation with a colleague. We had asked for two podia so that we could each stand behind one to help in the theatrics of our double-header. Alas, when we arrived at the venue, there was one superb podium with a neon light winding its way up the outside – something they might have borrowed from a nightclub for all we knew. The other was simply plain wood. But no matter. When it was time for us to come on stage, my colleague, who had positioned herself behind the nightclub podium, was suitably introduced. Then the MC introduced me by saying, 'And here's Brian, who has brought his own neon with him'. For a long time afterwards, people could recall exactly what I had worn that day, while some might have had trouble remembering just who it was who had been performing with me!

Sometimes, if we haven't been to the venue before, it can pay to bring along two outfits – one dark, and the other lighter. Wearing a dark suit in front of a dark background can make us blend into the surroundings – not a particularly clever thing to do if we are trying to stand out from the crowd. But we have already remarked on the fact that darker clothes tend to add a touch of formality. If we don't have a lighter suit, we can always consider what colour of shirt to wear to offset the dark suit. A crisp white shirt, or even yellow or pink could look extremely professional, depending on whether you can carry it off. (My wife squirms at the very thought of some of the colour combinations I have come up with – not helped by a touch of colour blindness I have in the pink to purple part of the spectrum; but even she had to admit that I certainly looked the part when I occasionally read the news on television wearing a pink shirt – but only when I was also wearing a dark suit and a colour-coordinated tie!)

Women, I always think in this respect, have it easier. They can get away with a smart casual look where a man might be forced into the situation of wearing a suit. And they can wear a variety of colours that their male colleagues might have difficulty getting away with!

Male or female, we should make sure that our outfit is a comfortable fit. There should be no pens, mobile phones or loose change in our pockets as they can create nasty bulges and spoil the overall crisp lines of the effect we are trying to project.

Women should go for dark colours too, and wear either trousers or long skirts. Short skirts create the wrong impression, while plunging necklines can also detract from that air of gravitas that they are trying to project. Keep patterns to a minimum as they can distract the audience. Jewellery should be subtle and not claim the audience's attention at the expense of what is being said.

Ready for the off

And finally … after all the preparation … finally it is time to draw breath, wait for the audience to file in, collect our thoughts, and prepare to be a star!

Summary

- Choosing the right room for the ambience we are trying to create is essential.
- Think how best to position the audience.
- Make sure that lighting and sound systems are adjusted to best advantage.
- The position of a slide projector can be crucial.
- Take care over the positioning of power and video cables.
- Wear appropriate clothing.

INSTANT TIP

Take nothing for granted. Check in plenty of time that everything needed is there and that it works!

08

What techniques should I use for engaging the audience?

The big day has arrived. We have been introduced to the delegates; the topic of our speech has been mentioned. From this point on, we are the main focus of attention. We are on our own!

This is where we start our performance – not just a question of getting into our speech as quickly as possible, but mentally preparing both ourselves, and the audience too, for what we are about to impart.

A sense of the dramatic is called for. It is not just a collection of words that we will be using; like any performance it will involve the use of movement, passion, eye contact, dramatic pause, and many other techniques used by actors every day of their working lives. And this is where the thespian in us, which I talked about in an earlier chapter, must rise to the fore.

For some people, this is the hardest part. They are not 'born actors' and find that putting on a sense of the dramatic does not come naturally. The danger, too, is that by 'trying too hard' to be thespians they actually come across as ham actors – lacking sincerity and thereby losing credibility. In this regard, everyone has to discover their own comfort zone and act in a style that is both comfortable and sounds natural. Getting a close friend or companion to listen through and advise on how we are doing can be invaluable in this regard.

When our name is called out by the MC – if indeed that is what is happening on this particular occasion – we should look cool, calm and collected, yet eager and excited that we have been honoured simply by being asked to talk. When our name is announced, we should all but jump out of that seat and walk purposely to the podium – but not too fast – our head held high, our shoulders back, a smile on our face.

We look round the audience. We should wait for silence; absolute silence so that we can hear that proverbial pin dropping. Never be afraid of long silences. They add drama. They heighten tension. And at the very start they add to the overall expectation of a star performance.

The start is crucial. This is where we can either capture the inner souls of our audience or lose them completely. We can gain their confidence; or we can fall at the very first fence. We can get them hanging on to our every word; or we can warn them of approaching boredom. Which is it to be?

The voice

Talking to a roomful of people is not the same as having a two-way conversation with a close friend. With a one-on-one we can see the visual cues from our listener and know that they understand what we are saying and we can temper our message or alter our flow if the signs are that we are not getting through.

We don't have that luxury in the company of a lot of people; and the voice must therefore be used differently if we are to ensure that our audience remains on our wavelength.

Ever since the Tower of Babel, language has been at the heart of communication. We have all learned to talk from birth and we all think we are terribly good at it. What could be more natural or easier than something we've all done since day one? Unfortunately, the reality is different. Most of us don't have to cogitate very long to think of people we know who are anything but good communicators.

There are several reasons or categories they fall into – noting that the first three are personal and may not always be correctable, but do cause misunderstandings:

- Speech impediment – whatever its cause, this is bound to create a difficulty in comprehension by others.
- Not using their mother tongue, which leads to the use of inappropriate tenses, declensions and conjugations.
- Strong regional accents or differences in the use of language on a regional basis.

The correctable areas, which need to be addressed, are:

- Talking in jargon – which most specialist groups tend to do.
- Talking *at* the person with whom we are trying to communicate – but communication, by definition, is a two-way process.
- Malapropisms or misuse of the language out of ignorance.
- Highfalutin or inappropriate use of long or impressive-sounding words in order to gain the upper ground – we all know this is simply a load of floccinaucinihilipilification!

It's awful to have a communication problem but the problem is that most of us don't think we have one! Jargon apart, though, many people have difficulty making themselves heard. They mumble or talk too quietly; they don't project; they're afraid of coming over as too domineering.

Facets of good speaking

To use the voice to best effect in a presentation involves us having to put a great deal of effort into the way we manipulate it.

- Confidence is a key facet. If our audience doesn't believe in us, then why will they bother giving us the time of day, let alone sit through our presentation?

- Conviction in what we are saying is also key. Putting across our passion, despite the fact that we are genuinely convinced in our own argument, can cause our audience to doubt us and put question marks over what we have to say.
- Enthusiasm, too, is essential. If we are confident and are convinced in our own arguments, then very likely we will also come across as enthused. Being enthusiastic is also infectious. If we sound all fired up by what we have to say, the chances are we will have an easier 'sell in' of our ideas than if we appear not so turned on by the subject matter in hand.
- Our integrity is also something that must never be brought into question. If we try to bluff our way through a sticky patch, we can be sure the audience will almost certainly catch us out with the result that nearly everything else we say may also be challenged.
- Of course, if we can show we have a widespread grasp of the subject in hand by being able to show off our knowledge, then that too is very important, though not necessarily essential. Or is it? Broadcasters must often talk about a subject with which they are not very familiar. After all, not every broadcaster can be well versed in every subject. But the fact that they have done their research thoroughly gives them the wherewithal to ask searching questions of their interviewees and, as such, shows them to be 'instant experts'!
- Finally, having a good voice is certainly a valuable asset, but is hardly essential to a good

presentation. Few are blessed with really beautiful voices, but there are thousands more who are good presenters.

Being heard clearly

If an audio system is available then, assuming it has been set up correctly, it should help to make us more audible, especially for those at the back of the room. However, if there is none available it is essential that we project our voice as clearly and loudly as possible.

This is not something that everyone can do naturally. It can take a lot of practice; but the main things to remember are to keep our head up, to slow down in our delivery, to open our mouths wider than we might be comfortable with in normal speech, and to enunciate our consonants.

Having a good posture can help enormously in this since it aids breathing and we therefore have enough air to take us to the end of a sentence … rather than … having to breathe … in the middle of … a sentence! Remember to breathe sensibly, taking in a full breath at a full stop and topping up your reservoir at a comma.

Many people use air from the top of their lungs, but this is not using our chest capacity to advantage. Look at the difference in the way that opera singers project their voices compared with the majority of pop singers who simply wouldn't be heard without the aid of a microphone pushed half way down their throats. The difference is often as a result of posture – the opera singer breathes all the way down to her diaphragm while the pop diva takes lots of little breaths and whispers into her microphone.

Good posture can help enormously in our delivery. If we remain upright with our shoulders slightly back and slow down our delivery from what would normally feel comfortable in everyday use, we should be able to be heard at the back of a room without the need for amplification.

Vary the voice range

If we listen to any professional speaker – really good TV presenters are an ideal source from whom we can learn – we can hear the way they don't just speak at one pace and at one pitch. They speed up or slow down, commensurate with the excitement present in their subject matter; they raise or lower the pitch of their voice such that low tones emphasise what they are saying, while the high notes convey urgency. Volume should remain more constant, but again a sudden drop in the level of the voice can add significance, as in an aside to the audience in a Shakespearean drama.

We all have a tremendous range of expressions inherent in our voices. They are there for a purpose, and for every presentation we should aim to use these expressions as much as possible.

What we do need to be wary of is the speed of our delivery. It is very common for people feeling nervous to speed up when they talk and the result can sometimes appear as a gabble. Ideally a rate of around 150 words per minute is comfortable for an audience. Too slow and we can send them to sleep; too fast and we can lose their concentration or make it hard for them to keep up with us.

A useful technique is to pause slightly longer than we might feel naturally comfortable with at the end of paragraphs to give our audience a chance to catch up with our mental road map.

This can be especially effective if we are using PowerPoint slides: we pause as we change the slide, then turn back to the audience and start to speak again. It feels natural and says to the audience in no uncertain terms, 'I'm in control!'

One of the reasons mentioned earlier about not reading from our script is that, if we do so, our presentation could sound flat and uninspired. When we are seen as talking off the cuff, using natural expressions and with a natural rise and fall to our voices, we are much more likely to sound spontaneous, for that in effect is what we are. If we want to sound convincing, then we should be convincing and that means using the whole gamut of emotions – happy, sad, cheerful, intriguing, confidential – whatever the emotion, we should not be afraid of employing every technique available to us. And, strange as it may seem, a smile can actually improve your voice. Even if you are talking about something serious or emotional, imagining a smile at the back of your throat helps to lift the tenor of the voice and make it more comprehensible.

At the same time, it is possible to change the entire meaning of a phrase by the way it is said. Think, for instance, of that simple word 'OK' – derived from the American GIs in the Second World War to mean All Correct. This, in theory can mean 'Sure. I agree with you.' But what if it is slightly drawn out with a high rise to the voice? 'O-kay! I'm 100 per cent behind what you are saying.'

But change that to a long drawn-out O-kay with a

question mark in your voice and it could mean 'I'm not sure I totally agree with you.' Again, said simply and it can mean 'I hear what you are saying, but I'll think about whether I agree with you or not.'

The same problem can arise with the incorrect inflection used by some speakers. Most of us will have come across people who make every statement sound like a question; and although this can sometimes be the result of a national way of speaking (Australians, for instance, are well known for this) it can really confuse those who are not used to this particular way of talking.

So if we can transform the meanings of individual words so easily, think how we can alter the meanings of overall sentences and cause total confusion simply by the way we say what we want to put across.

The use of strong words

It is a truism that the use of some words can portray us as strong and credible, while others give the impression that we're indecisive or, worse still, out-and-out liars.

Many words convey doubt – *possibly, suggest, try, as soon as possible* – to name but a few. What if instead we used *definitely, recommend, will,* or *immediately* – just think how we would come over as much more positive in our speech.

We can even take this one stage further. It is not for nothing that the army teaches its NCOs to use active rather than passive words. To come over as authoritative we don't want to sound passive, and this comes across in the type of words we use.

So, the secret here is to 'tell it like it is'. *I made a mistake* sounds much more as if we are in control, compared to *a mistake has been made* – even though we are admitting it was our fault!

Likewise, which would you think comes across as more authoritative: *a 50 per cent sales increase will be achieved* or *we will achieve growth of over 50 per cent*? Being active in our language implies we have conviction in our actions and this will gain us more credibility with our audience.

Warm-up exercises

Most athletes wouldn't dream of entering a race without warming up beforehand. To use their muscles to best effect means getting those muscles out of their slumbers and putting them through their paces before the actual race itself.

Voice delivery is no different!

I usually go through a fixed routine whenever I have to give a speech, or go on-air or undertake some other form of public speaking. First I yawn two or three times – this stretches the mouth. (Think of all those shots of hippopotami on natural history programmes which invariably show them doing this better than any animal on earth!)

Next I wiggle my bottom jaw backwards and forwards a few times. (I usually try to find somewhere private such as a WC cubicle, since I don't want to scare off my audience!)

And then I practise some tongue twisters to get my tongue loosened up so that I can 'get my tongue round' almost any word without any problems. I usually repeat the tongue twister two or three times, speeding up each time until I literally cannot go any faster.

Everyone has their favourites. Mine are:

Peter Piper Picked a Peck of Pickled Peppers;
A Peck of Pickled Peppers Peter Piper Picked;
If Peter Piper Picked that Peck of Pickled Peppers,
Where's the Peck of Pickled Peppers Peter Piper Picked?

Or

Many an anemone has an enemy anemone.

Or even

Can you imagine an imaginary menagerie manager
Imagining managing an imaginary menagerie?

Use the audience for dramatic effect

One particular technique that works wonders in any presentation is to involve the audience. Think of when we converse with a friend. Unless we are extremely self-centred, the chances are that we don't just talk and leave all the listening to the other person. We ask questions, we seek verbal as well as visual confirmation, we pause and we use rhetorical questions to improve the communication process.

And so it is with our presentation. Rhetorical questions are wonderful at creating drama, especially when employed with a long pause afterwards. 'Why do you think so-and-so happened?' we ask, looking around the audience, who will normally be unlikely to respond. <*long pause*> 'It's because … ' and off we trot on to the next theme of our exposition.

We shouldn't be afraid of using facial expressions as we use the rhetorical question either. It might be appropriate to stare into the distance as we 'try' to find the answer to our own question and then smile as we 'find' the correct answer! We could look quizzically at several members of the audience too, just so long as we don't embarrass them by lingering too long holding their gaze.

Above all else, enthusiasm is infectious. It also can make up for a whole load of other deficiencies and, if we sound enthusiastic, the chances are that our audience will be similarly enthused.

Another way to raise enthusiasm is to move around the stage. As a general rule of thumb, we can move around when we want to involve the audience in some way, such as asking rhetorical questions; but when we want the emphasis to shift back to us, we should simply stay put.

Of course, this works far better in large rooms with large audiences than for small-scale presentations where if we walk around a lot we can end up driving our audience crazy. Generally we should aim to appear purposeful in our movements, not random.

One particularly effective use of this technique is when we are changing the focus of our presentation. Walking across the room saying absolutely nothing can be dramatic, while also signalling to the audience that we are moving on in our subject matter.

Speaking with our bodies

It has been shown in many studies that the use of body language is very important when giving presentations. When I say 'the use of body language', this might imply a conscious element of leading the audience. But most body language is often totally automatic, and 'gives the person away' sometimes without them even knowing it. In fact, it has even been suggested that as much as 90 per cent of face-to-face communication is non-verbal.

Much has been researched and written on the use of body language, and what is very clear is that it is almost always noticed by an audience even if they are unaware that they are picking up these visual cues from the way we present ourselves.

By the term 'body language', we can be referring to a number of things. How we position ourselves, what we do with our hands, our eye contact with the audience, gestures and mannerisms. All will be giving off signals that will affect the way in which other people perceive us.

By learning the secrets of body language – how to reassure our audience that we are credible, trustworthy and knowledgeable – we can dramatically help our overall presentation, while at the same time glean useful feedback from the delegates who – if we have learned to interpret their non-verbal signals – will often show what they are feeling without saying a word.

(A really useful reference on body language can be found in the same *Instant Manager* series as this book: *Body Language* by Geoff Ribbens and Greg Whitear.)

So before we have even opened our mouth, we need to think about how we are going to stand. Feet slightly apart, perhaps one leg slightly in front of the other, will ensure we do not rock from one leg to the other. Equally, though, we should be wary of being seen as static and inanimate since this can make us appear aloof and unfriendly. Being rooted to one spot doesn't add to an overall impression of enthusiasm, and if we aren't enthusiastic about our presentation, then how can we expect anyone else to be?

Casual body language is a non-starter if we want to tell our audience that what we are about to say really matters. Our voice, too, needs to be appropriate for the occasion. So there are plenty of things to think about, but whatever we do, we must get off to a good start.

I always think it's a bit like conducting an orchestra. If you've ever been to a classical concert, you will know that the conductor doesn't just walk on stage and start straight into the music. No. He walks on purposefully; he strides up to the podium; he waits for silence; he eyes his musicians, making contact with each and every one of them at the same time, getting them into the mood of the music before it has actually begun; he waits for the audience to quieten down; he lets them know he is in control; he raises his baton, pauses for a moment, and the music begins!

Just as our voices can give away so much of what we feel inside and what lies behind what we are trying to convey, so too can our bodies give away a lot about how comfortable or self-conscious or confident we are.

It can be a very good idea when rehearsing our presentation to use a video camera to record what we look like. Many people are surprised how well they come across and this can be a useful ego booster when our feelings of insecurity are most likely to rise to the fore. At the same time we can look out for non-verbal signals that we might wish to change or add.

'All the world's a stage'

Our presentation is a drama and it is our job to be a thespian – to act the part; to raise expectations; to get our audience onto our wavelength; to win them over with our performance and our arguments; and to get them believing in us, to take on board the message we are trying to convey; to believe in us.

Some speakers find it works well to make their opening remarks with their arms open as if they were about to embrace someone. It can make the audience immediately feel as if we are opening out to them and making them inclusive of, rather than purely spectators to, the presentation. The whole point here is to establish an instant rapport with the delegates and open-hand gestures can indicate honesty, sincerity and openness.

One thing we must never do is to start with an apology. We shouldn't be sounding cocky or brash, but we should be exuding confidence; otherwise why should we expect anyone to sit up and take notice of what we are saying?

This feeling of confidence is something that should permeate our entire performance. We also need the audience to feel a common bond with our objectives, so a feeling of empathy, of shared emotions is something that we must develop as the presentation moves forward.

As we rehearsed our presentation we will have practised where we should inject elements of humour, of pathos, or passion and enthusiasm – but we should be wary of overdoing any of these emotions. The phrase 'practised sincerity' comes to mind, but really there is no substitute for appearing natural yet enthusiastic about our subject.

The use of humour, if we are not natural humorists, can be fraught with danger. A joke or witticism told well can make a presentation memorable; but inexpertly used, humour can be a killer for any speech. Telling old jokes, telling funny jokes badly or telling unfunny jokes can lose us our audience, not to mention the danger of offending some of those present if we verge into areas of race, politics or religion. We must know our abilities in this field and if in any doubt the maxim should be to leave it out.

Think where to stand

We have already remarked that where we position ourselves in the room is vital to the success of the presentation. Everyone must be able to see us, of course, but we also need to be able to see our notes, be able to interact with our visual aids and be well placed for any microphone that is picking us up.

For these reasons, it is often a good idea to use a podium or lectern if one is available. We can use it for our notes; it might be possible for extra lighting to be made available making legibility easier too; there could be a clock provided, or we could place our watch down so that we can judge the timing of the speech.

If no lectern is available, then standing in the middle of the platform – or slightly to the side if we are using slides – is a natural choice. But standing is usually better than sitting down if we want to be seen and be heard and it also emphasises the importance of what we are doing. In this regard, it is not for nothing that so many international TV stations now get their news anchors to deliver the news standing up.

On the other hand, it could also be appropriate to sit down if our aim is to be informal, or to gain maximum feedback from our audience. Invariably when I am giving training courses I sit down at, or near, the speaker's table, so positioned that everyone can see me, but also giving the visual cue that we are a roomful of equals (with me, perhaps, the first among the equals!).

The use of a lectern is also to be recommended for those of us who are nervous, since we can place our hands unobtrusively on each corner so that, instead of being embarrassed about what to do with our hands, they have a natural home as we are presenting. Failing that, the most natural place for our hands is by our sides, but never in our pockets.

Using our hands in a meaningful way

Some have argued that having hands in pockets shows disrespect to the audience, or that it implies a degree of over-informality. Actually, there is an even more important reason not to put hands in pockets. To do so stops us using what amounts to a powerful body language tool in getting our points across in a credible manner.

Hands are useful for emphasising particular messages. If we think of the way that southern Europeans especially tend to use their hands in everyday gestures, they can emphasise a particular point; and in presentational techniques they can also be used for directing attention to a particular feature. Two-handed gestures often work better than the use of one hand – for instance in using the two hands as scales to show one side of the argument against the other side of that argument.

Whatever we do, though, such gestures should look natural. They should be meaningful so that they match the content of our presentation, for if they appear arbitrary they can undermine credibility in what we are saying. Above all, hand gestures work better if they are made slowly and deliberately – a bit like moving one's hand through water – rather than in a jerky movement that is over before the audience has even cottoned on to the fact that it has been made.

It is also important that we don't simply use the same gesture over and over again, for we can guarantee that to do so will get our audience waiting for that same gesture to be made, a bit like a game, rather than listening to what it is we have to say.

There is a much-watched TV station in the Arabian Gulf that had obviously brought in some guru to train their TV news anchors how to present on air. I used to find myself spellbound every time I watched this evening bulletin simply waiting for one particular gesture from whoever was reading the news that night. It didn't matter who the news anchor was; the same gesture of a hand being offered out to the audience as he or she ran through what items were coming up after the commercial break could be guaranteed to be made. It turned into classic comedy as the presenters themselves obviously believed they were being smart by having remembered this little tip. If only they had bothered to watch a recording of themselves afterwards!

Similarly, we should never try to emphasise anything by pointing at the audience. Pointing can be taken as rude, and it is simply not worth the risk of alienating people by doing so.

Whatever we do, though, there is no room for fiddling with jewellery, pens or keys; we should avoid wiping sweaty hands on our trousers; and, obviously, we should never scratch *anywhere* – as I once saw a world famous architect do as she faced the world's press talking about one of her creations. It was a hot and humid day, and the fact that she was somewhat overweight added to the amount of sweat on her brow; but she also had the audience spellbound as she painstakingly scratched little bits of her anatomy at every conceivable opportunity. As one of the photographers for a national newspaper remarked, there was hardly a moment during the entire presentation that he could get a decent picture of her!

Whether we are standing or sitting, the thing to remember above all is that casual body language is inappropriate for the seriousness of what we are trying to achieve. Don't confuse casual with relaxed! To appear relaxed can put people at their ease; to appear casual implies that we are not taking the subject or event seriously.

Worse still, some people slouch when giving a presentation in the standing up position. Instead of holding their shoulders back like a tin soldier, they allow themselves to roll forward and collapse from their middles. This has two effects, both of which we want to avoid: firstly it tends to reduce the flow of air so we tend to become breathy and speak in a low volume. Secondly, the body language is screaming out to the audience, 'Hey guys. I really don't feel comfortable standing up in front of you and talking to you.'

It is always a useful exercise to watch politicians speak, since many of them have had considerable training in body language techniques. It was George Burns who is famously quoted as saying, 'The secret of acting is sincerity. If you can fake that, you've got it made!' Well, for sheer 'practised sincerity' it is hard to beat what politicians come up with. (Never trust a politician, I was always told in my earlier days. They are so well rehearsed in coming across as sincere, caring, people that you have to wonder why they don't all become second-hand car salesman when their days in politics are over!) For most of them, it obviously works; and so if it works for them, why don't we copy some of their techniques and see if we can't emulate their success in public speaking?

Eye contact

Eye contact is also something that makes a lasting impression on our audience. Think of someone who always looks away when speaking to us. What message do they give out about themselves? That they are nervous? Or perhaps untrustworthy? The very things we are trying *not* to communicate to our audience.

Likewise, think of a successful TV presenter. Almost always they are looking at us – the audience – straight through that camera lens and directly into our eyes. Yet sometimes, things go wrong. A faulty instruction from the gallery and they could be looking into another camera. They have 'lost us'. They are no longer holding our attention, but are talking to someone else. Something as simple as that can have a huge impact on the audience. In fact there is a trend nowadays for many a news bulletin to end with a distant camera shot of the presenter seemingly putting away his pen, closing his computer prompt and shuffling his paper script back into order. The implication is clear. He has finished talking to us and is ready for the 'off'.

So it is vital that we maintain eye contact with members of the audience in order to hold their attention and establish a rapport with them.

As a rule of thumb, we should aim to spend at least half our time in direct eye contact with members of the audience – not just one or two individuals, and especially not just the attractive members of the opposite sex. Some will be more responsive to what we are saying than others, and it is often more comfortable concentrating our eye contact with these people; but we should aim to include each and every member of the audience at least once or twice in our eye contact throughout the presentation if at all possible.

Sometimes, however, this is simply not possible because either there is a spotlight shining directly at us, or the audience is sitting in the dark or in low lighting conditions, in which case we should make eye contact with specific areas where we know the audience to be and make out that that particular blind spot is someone with whom we are specifically trying to communicate.

A variation of this is to use what is known as the *W-M* technique. By tracing the letter W with our eyes across the audience, and then following this as if we are tracing the letter M, the effect is that we are taking in all members of the audience and making them feel included.

Again, think what a professional TV presenter does: although she cannot see her audience, she imagines she is talking to someone sitting right inside the camera lens and the result is that each and every member of her audience sitting at home feels she is talking individually to them.

An even more important reason for eye contact is that it gives us an immediate reaction gauge of our audience; for we can *see* if they are nodding off to sleep, if they have glazed expressions, if their concentration is wandering, if they are looking out of the windows or playing with their mobile phones. If we can instantly take on board these signals and modify our presentation accordingly, we can remedy a situation that is fast deteriorating, we can alter our speed of delivery, and we can concentrate on getting the message across far better than if we are running in auto-mode from a speech cast in stone.

Sometimes 'reading' our audience is essential, such as if we are presenting in the so-called 'grave-yard shift' –

that is immediately after a good long lunch – when we can almost guarantee that there will be at least one person starting to nod off.

In such circumstances I have found one of the best things to do is to walk in to the audience, raising my voice slightly. It should come across as if we are making an intimate point; but the change in acoustic and the increase in sound level will often be enough to wake the errant culprit without it appearing too obvious to everyone else!

Summary

- The start of a presentation is crucial. This is where we either capture or lose our audience completely.
- Variety in pace, volume and pitch of our voice adds interest and credibility to what we are saying.
- Exercise your jaw and lip muscles before speaking in public.
- Good eye contact should be maintained with our audience to make them feel included in the presentation rather than looking in from the outside.
- Don't confuse a casual posture with being relaxed.

INSTANT TIP

Non-verbal communication is often as important as what it is we are talking about.

09

How do I handle questions during and after the presentation?

To give a presentation without having a question and answer session (the famous Q&A) at the end would be like having fish without chips, or a cart without a horse. Some people find this the most difficult part of their performance, while others feel they can start to relax at this point and be their normal selves.

The point we should bear in mind – just as we have throughout the entire process of putting together our presentation – is that preparation pays dividends, and this is especially true at this part of the event.

For instance, when we researched the make up and needs of our audience, this should have given us an understanding of the kind of questions they would be likely to raise. It means to a large extent we should be able to anticipate the actual questions themselves.

In addition, it is possible that we can get an idea of who the main protagonists within the audience are likely to be and whether they will be basically on our side, or trying to score points off us.

Perhaps our audience is made up of a particular grouping – a board from Human Resources, or a sales team, for example – and any 'inside' information we can glean about them may also be much to our advantage at this stage.

When considering the actual presentation of our material, we saw that it was well worth over-preparing material so that we could have the luxury of dropping some, in order to make up time, but picking it up for use in the Q&A session. To be able to give anecdotal evidence as part of our answer in this session adds credibility to what we are saying, and reinforces our reputation of being able to talk off the cuff, as if we have not even prepared for this part!

So, as part of our preparation, it is worthwhile brainstorming the kind of questions that could be asked of us. By preparing for the difficult ones, especially for those that we would much rather not have to answer, we can go in to this part of the session feeling pretty confident. However, we should not forget, too, that many a presenter has flown through those difficult questions and then stumbled on the easy stuff simply because he has not felt it necessary to prepare these as thoroughly!

Another reason for preparing for difficult questions is that it gives us the chance to think up and rehearse anecdotal illustrations that can be recalled 'off the cuff', which again adds credibility and pizzazz to what we are talking about.

Honesty is always the best policy when presenting to a group. No one can know the answer to every question. It's how we handle such a situation that is so important. All good presenters have a range of techniques that work well for them and allow them to come out of a Q&A session 'smelling of roses'!

For instance, if we don't know the answer to a question, we could try tossing it back to the audience. 'Is there anyone here who has ever experienced that situation?' By effectively using the audience to help us, they will often enjoy their involvement because we are asking them to share their knowledge. But we must be sure to summarise what they have come up with and then add our own ideas (if we have any!). Offering a summary of their answers maintains our credibility and authority.

Another old standard is for us to say we will get back to the questioner with an answer. We should tell the questioner exactly when we will get back to them (preferably on the same day or, if that is not possible, as soon as possible after the event). Being open about this is much appreciated by the audience, just so long as we deliver on our promise!

Sometimes questions asked are simply too specific or too general to answer. But as the expert, we can take that question and ask a supplementary question in response. I was once giving a presentation on incorporating internet technologies into a business environment. Someone asked me a question to which I didn't know the answer. 'How do I set up my own DNS number,' he asked. Instead of admitting I didn't know the answer, I asked in reply 'what are you hoping to achieve by doing so?' He told me what his goal was – something that in fact had little to do with DNS number administration – and he was happy with my answer which never gave away my ignorance on that particular topic (but I learned very fast in case I was ever asked that question again!).

When should we allow questions?

Different presenters allow questions at different parts of the presentation; but although there is no right or wrong way, the majority of speakers take questions only at the end.

If we allow questions to be asked of us as and when they arise, it certainly aids informality – and this may be desirable if we are unsure of the level of knowledge of our audience. However, unless controlled carefully, we could find the subject veering off at a tangent and all our careful preparation in danger of flying out the window as we follow a path for which we had not planned.

Another method is to allow questions at the end of fixed sections of the presentation. For complex topics this could again be beneficial so that everyone has a chance to catch up before moving on to the next section.

If, however, our audience is large, or it is a formal occasion, we are likely to have little choice but to keep all questions to the end. It is certainly easier to control the flow of the overall talk and it is so commonplace that most people are comfortable with holding their questions back to the end. It also means we are better able to control the timing and flow of our speech and to keep ourselves on the straight and narrow.

In general, formal presentations will generate formal Q&As while informal sessions could encourage informal debate among a whole group of the audience.

The most important thing about the Q&A session, when held at the end, though, is that it will be the last thing that our audience remembers about our entire performance. If we gave a brilliant presentation, but stumbled over the answers at the end, the audience is likely to go away less than impressed. On the other hand, if we gave a mediocre performance in the speech itself, but shone like a star in the Q&As, it may be enough to save our reputation and allow us to leave with our head held high!

For this reason, many people choose to hold their Q&A sessions just before the end. The difference is a fine one; and the thinking goes along the following lines: what happens if the Q&As go badly, or if the audience turns hostile? Remember what we saw earlier – that the lasting memory of our audience as often as not will be how we ended our presentation. So some people hold the Q&A session just before the end, when they have said what they wanted to say, but before their killer close. This way, if the Q&As go badly, they still have a chance to pick up the pieces and to end their presentation with a bang.

It's up to you which you prefer to do; but think about it carefully, as if you are at all worried about your audience reaction, it could spell the difference between success and failure.

Getting the ball rolling

Something I often find when giving presentations is that come the Q&A session, when the audience is invited to ask whatever they like, there is absolute silence. No one wants to be the first to raise a hand; yet once the first question has been asked, there is no end of others wanting to add their voice to the general discussion.

I have invariably found that asking a friend in the audience to ask a simple question – one which I have obviously prepared well in advance – starts the ball rolling. If there is no one I know, I have asked a chairperson or MC to start off the Q&As instead.

Sometimes, though, exactly the opposite is the case. Someone may throw in a question when we don't want one. Here, if we were going to cover the point later on in the presentation anyway, we should thank the questioner, make it clear that we will come on to this point, and continue as before. If we weren't going to cover the area of concern, we could always say that this raises an important point, and that we'd be glad to explore this further at the end in the Q&A session.

When we are ready to take questions, we can signal that we really welcome them by using open body language, rather than folding our arms and standing back – that is almost guaranteed to stop anyone even thinking of asking us anything. Instead, we could walk towards the audience, perhaps sit down among them – if it is a small audience – or move away from the podium and use our voice to show that we really do want questions and feedback.

Why should the audience want to ask questions anyway?

A word of warning: we should never try to prejudge what it is the questioner is asking. It is all too easy to listen to the first half of the question and assume they want to know about a, b and c, when actually they were more interested in x, y and z.

Repeating the question so that others sitting at the back of the room, who might not have heard it properly, is also a good idea, and quite a legitimate way of buying thinking time in the process.

While the ostensible reason for asking a question is so that the questioner can clarify his thoughts or fill in a knowledge gap, we should also remember that some people may have different agendas. They may wish to put forward a different point of view, or even to show themselves off as experts to the assembled gathering.

Yet again, some people may not have properly thought through their question before they stand up to ask it, and what comes out is a mishmash of a number of questions all rolled into one. Here, the secret is to unravel what has been asked, answer the easiest part first (which gives us more thinking time) and then work our way through the different aspects of what has been asked.

There was a wonderful occasion I witnessed at an international film festival where the actress Susan Sarandon was giving a press conference. A Lebanese journalist, working for a lifestyle magazine, blurted out her question without, perhaps, properly thinking it through. 'Yesterday we met Jane Fonda, who [at 71] is very beautiful. But you, you have many wrinkles on your face. Are you happy with the way you look?' As I'm sure you can imagine, there was at first a very embarrassed and deafening silence until Ms Sarandon, being the consummate professional she undoubtedly is, smiled and came up with an answer about beauty emanating from within. At no point did she give any indication that she had been offended by the question and from that moment on, every single journalist in the room was fully on her side.

If the question being asked sounds trite or silly, we should never be tempted to put the questioner down. It may be, anyway, that we were not clear enough in what we were saying, and that the silly question is a reflection on what we said or did. If we remain polite at all times, answer in a professional manner and appear friendly and approachable at all times, we should have no difficulty in keeping the audience on side.

There will also be occasions when we may not actually wish to give out an answer to a particular question being asked. In this case it is perfectly acceptable to refuse to give an answer, just so long as we do it with good grace and give a clue as to why we do not want to answer. For instance, it may be that the question is all about something that is commercially confidential – journalists are always trying to find out such facts in press conferences, but they will understand if we tell them that this is the reason we can't or won't answer them and they won't think badly of us for answering this way.

It may be that we simply don't know the answer – in which case it never hurts to say so – but we could offer to look it up after the event and get back to the questioner. Again, no one expects anyone to know the answer to everything, so a careful refusal and explanation alienates no one. Of course, if we have a colleague in the audience who does know the answer to that particular question, it may be apposite for us to ask him to answer on our behalf. Having an expert to hand can be a very useful ploy!

One company I worked for used to stage annual road shows of its directors talking to staff among its many divisions spread across the north of England. Obviously the business couldn't simply grind to a halt as all staff members went to the road show. Instead, a summary of all the main points was put together into a staff newsletter, and if a question was asked to which the directors didn't know the answer, there would be an undertaking to publish the answer later in this newsletter. The staff felt they were being fairly treated as there was no attempt to hide the facts inherent in the answer.

Finally, we should neither go on too long with our answers, nor be so brief that we imply that we cannot be bothered to waste time on the poor questioner. We should keep eye contact for the initial part of our answer, and then widen our body language to include others in the room, too. This has two effects: it signals to the questioner that we don't want him to ask an inexhaustible supply of questions when others might have questions they want to ask, and it also means we don't lose the concentration of the majority of the audience who may start to sag if we give undue attention to one person only.

Summary

- Q&A sessions are a highly effective way of closing a presentation.
- The majority of speakers take questions only at the end of their presentation.
- We should be honest if we don't know the answer, and if we cannot answer we should give a reason why we cannot or will not.
- We should remain in control throughout the Q&A session rather than letting it lapse into a free-for-all.

INSTANT TIP

Preparation for the Q&As is as important as preparing for the speech itself.

10

What problems am I likely to encounter and how can I deal with them?

Throughout this book we have been considering the importance of preparation – preparation in all things pertaining to our presentation, including the speech itself, the visual aids, our notes, research on our audience, and so on.

Now let's hold on there a moment; for audiences are made up of all types of people. Some are the quiet type; some are aggressive; yet others are eager to show off how much *they* know and, unfortunately, there are also those – admittedly rare – whose only intention appears to be to make trouble for us.

We need also to be aware that there are genuine reasons why some people tend to switch off in presentations. The most obvious cause is that they may genuinely not want to be there in the first place. Perhaps they feel we are there to convey bad news, or they feel that our presentation is simply a distraction from a very heavy workload. They will be determined not to like our presentation, however much of a star we are. And they are easy to spot: sitting as often as not with arms folded and looking continually impatient. It may be we can win them over; but at the end of the day it might also be worthwhile considering asking them to leave; for we don't want their negativity affecting the rest of the delegates.

Some, of course, might have been bored into submission by previous speakers; and this is quite an easy thing to fix. If we start off with a killer opening and win their attention from the very beginning, then we will present ourselves as such a contrast from the previous speakers, and as such a relief, that they should quickly come over to our side!

Then there are those who know a great deal already of what we are talking about. That may be unavoidable since everyone needs to be brought up to speed so that we are able to relate on a common footing. But if we see a problem in the making here, the best thing is to acknowledge that some people may already be ahead of the game and simply ask for their patience while we bring everyone's knowledge up to the same level.

Be prepared!

In business presentations, instances of troublemakers sitting in our audience are, thankfully, rare indeed. But if we have been deliberately controversial, or there is a high chance there will be dissatisfied members of the audience, then we have to be prepared.

Sometimes we can see them coming a mile off: they will ask difficult or awkward questions; they will sit there looking bored or disapproving; they might be sarcastic.

And, once again, that magic phrase *body language* comes to the fore. An effective presenter should always be tuned in to the body language of the audience, especially where that body language is negative, or downright hostile. Such indications might need to be faced head-on and brought out into the open, rather than leaving the dissatisfied people smouldering for whatever reason they may feel they have.

One of the most common defensive postures is for someone to sit with arms folded and perhaps even with ankles crossed. Although many people use crossed arms as a relaxing position, it can be a good indicator of who in the room feels threatened by something we may have said or done. Those, for instance, who cross their arms if we criticise something that is dear to them are straight away giving us very useful feedback that we are treading on sensitive ground and that we had better find out what it is they disagree with.

Other tell-tale signs of disagreement are when an audience member starts picking pieces of imaginary fluff from her jacket, or perhaps gives a slight shake of the head while looking straight at the speaker. We should keep an eye open, for there are valuable cues there for all to see.

If their behaviour actually turns into heckling, then we should be prepared for them. First and foremost a witty riposte might be the best solution. No matter how obnoxious they are, if we can keep the audience on our side by seemingly allowing the most crass questions or comments to float over our head, we will have done well. Humour can often diffuse the most unpleasant of situations, just so long as we never resort to sarcasm or scoring cheap points off our opponent.

The other extreme is to treat the question as serious and give it a full answer without getting at all flapped by the fact that the questioner is trying to irritate us. We should certainly never imply that the question or questioner is being stupid or deliberately provocative. Eventually the rest of the audience may chip in and keep the obnoxious person at bay – and we will have risen in their estimation in the process. Were we to put the questioner down, however, the audience will invariably side with the questioner – irrespective of how obnoxious he is.

Are there any tips on how I should retaliate?

Sometimes it pays simply to ignore a heckler as if he wasn't there. Again, the audience may take it upon themselves to quieten the miscreant; at the same time we must be careful to ensure that if we have lost the attention of some audience members during this period, we reiterate any important points that they might have missed in order that they should not be left behind.

On the other hand, if the heckler is creating too much nuisance, it may be appropriate to ask the stewards – if there are any – to throw the heckler out, or 'please show him the door' in polite language!

There was the famous case in 1988 when the BBC TV news anchor Sue Lawley remained totally unruffled when four lesbian protesters broke into the BBC's Six O'Clock news studio while she was on air, protesting against new laws that banned local councils from promoting homosexuality.

While Lawley did her best to continue presenting the show, her co-presenter Nicholas Witchell was left to sit on, and muffle, one of the protestors who had handcuffed herself to the newsdesk.

'We have rather been invaded,' she said, as she continued to read the news while the protesters handcuffed themselves to bits of studio equipment. That incident, and Lawley's total professionalism in carrying on almost as if nothing had happened, has never been forgotten by the British public and earned her widespread respect for many years after.

So, in short, we should never retaliate towards a difficult member of the audience. The temptation might indeed be very great, but if we can keep our cool, the audience will think better of us for it and an ugly scene will be less likely, which no one wants. Further, if we did retaliate, the entire event could degenerate into a mud-slinging or verbal slanging match.

Perhaps a heckler wants to present a point of view that is diametrically opposite to what we are trying to present? Again we should not argue. Instead it will come across much better if we acknowledge the question or point being raised, and then ask them to reconsider what we have had to say; and if they wish to discuss it with us *after* the presentation we will be happy to oblige.

Another really annoying situation occurs when two or more people appear to be chatting away, not listening to what we have to say and, worse still, disrupting others in the process. Now, it could be that they have a problem with understanding what it is we have said, in which case this could be a signal that is giving us due warning to bring them up to speed on what we are trying to put across.

On the other hand, they may simply be gossiping between themselves on some totally unrelated topic. If it becomes distracting either for ourself or other members of the audience, it may be best to stop talking, wait for them to stop (very often they will become extremely embarrassed at this point) and ask if they have any questions about what we have just said.

Keeping them awake!

Sometimes we will have drawn the short straw and found we have been asked to give our presentation in the graveyard shift – that infamous time just after lunch when the phenomenon of audience members nodding off to sleep is a well-known hazard.

There are some simple things we can do to counteract this situation. Sometimes all that is required is to change the sound of our voice or use a strong gesture to emphasise a point, perhaps moving into the audience a little. This will often have the required effect, though it may be only a temporary solution and those nodding off will start down their weary path once more.

We could try mentioning them by name, perhaps asking a question of them; but if we do this it may be best to mention the sleepy delegate's name only as the third person to be asked, or else the rest of the delegates will quickly guess what we are up to!

Another way is to get the audience to raise their hands to show they are in agreement with a particular point we have just made. Or we could make a point of mentioning particular people in the audience where possible, such as, 'Simone, here, was telling me earlier on that she is allergic to peanuts' and this could then trigger others to be alert in case their name is mentioned.

Finally, if we have been talking for a while and people in the audience start to look bored, it is sometimes better to cut our losses and move on to another topic, or else to highlight that the point we are getting to is important and hope that some sit up and take notice.

Are there any special tips when presenting to young people?

Although you may think the chances of having to present to young people are unlikely to come your way, you might just be surprised. It may be you will be asked to speak to a group of school leavers about your particular profession; you might be involved with youth project work; or find yourself having to key up brand new members of your organisation.

Interacting with young people can be very different from doing so with more mature adults. For one thing, they tend to openly express their feelings when adults might try to cover up what they feel out of embarrassment. It isn't that they are trying to be rude. It's just that they refuse to pretend what they don't genuinely feel.

At the same time, young people can come across as shallow or insincere when in reality, though seemingly untouched superficially, they experience genuine emotion below the surface.

This sometimes translates into the way they react to what is being said. It is not necessarily the cold hard facts that will stir them into action, rather than the fact that the person speaking to them is genuine and can speak from the heart. In fact it is sometimes the people who are regarded as poor presenters to other adults around them who come over the best with young people as the value judgements are made from a different perspective.

The best language for interaction is simple language. Uncommon or difficult words can leave listeners confused and at times even insulted. But whereas more mature people will simply get over this, young people can feel a sense of resentment.

Audience participation invariably is an important element in presenting to young people. They won't hesitate to ask questions that most adults wouldn't dream of asking. *How much money do you earn?* or *Have you ever fired someone?* are commonplace questions. Whenever you see politicians playing for votes by visiting a youth club or school, hone in on the questions being asked of them. They can provide much amusement if the said politician isn't aware of this most basic of youthful behaviour!

The youth of today tend to be very much more world-savvy than their parents' generation. With mass media and internet technologies playing an increasingly important part of their everyday lives, many so-called kids will have the edge on their seniors; so any condescending speech will go down with them like the proverbial lead balloon.

And finally, whatever you do, you should never try to be 'one of the lads' with younger people. Think back to when you were ten years old. You thought that 15 was ancient. At 18 you desperately wanted to be 21. By the time you reached 21 you still thought 30 was old and that 40 was ancient. And so it goes on throughout your life. Many of us more senior members of society still feel that inside we are at least 20 years younger, if only our bodies weren't so judgemental! Alas, most young people are too. So the lesson to be learned is to act your age: your real age, not what you think you feel like inside. Any attempt to be one of them will simply backfire.

Things we absolutely, definitely, 100 per cent shouldn't say

Believe it or not, there are some people who dig themselves into the most frightful holes simply for want of not having thought through properly what they want to say, or because they become a jumble of nerves and say the very first thing that comes into their heads.

If we want the audience to believe in us, then they have to have confidence in us; so there is no room for apologising to them if things start to go wrong. If equipment malfunctions, if we have been held up unavoidably in heavy traffic, or the caterers haven't been able to organise the coffee break properly, we must still appear to be in total control.

And being in total control means not admitting that we haven't had time to prepare properly, or appearing hesitant before them, or even so much as suggesting that we weren't born and brought up to believe that public speaking is our entire *raison d'être*. I have even heard some people admit to their audiences that they would rather be somewhere else instead of standing up and talking to them. So if they don't want to be there, why on earth should the audience bother?

Another common no-no, and one that is so easily done, is to get the names of key people wrong. Sometimes our mind goes a total blank at the key moment; it happens to us all. Just watch the annual Oscars ceremony on television if you want to enjoy the embarrassment that others face when they cannot remember the names of their co-stars or directors! In which case we should make light of it, perhaps describing ourselves as having just gone through a 'senior moment'. But never should we take a stab in the dark hoping that we'll almost get it right. Saying nothing is better than saying the wrong name.

What do I do if the equipment fails?

Dealing with temperamental equipment during a presentation is bound to cause intense frustration, but if this ever happens, we should stay relaxed and firmly in control if we are to keep the audience on side. Many problems are associated with loose connections or connections that have worked their way free at some point, and very often simply checking the leads, such as the wire between the monitor output on our laptop computer and the input on the projector, will solve the problem instantly.

If checking the leads for a loose connection doesn't work, it might be necessary to switch off the equipment and to reboot it. Due to the vagaries of computers, especially those that are Windows-based, this will often solve the problem.

Sometimes, at major events, all the speakers are asked to send in copies of their slides in advance so that they can all be set up on one computer and be instantly accessible by everyone. Well, if this is asked of you, by all means comply with the request, but I would urge you to take a back-up copy of the slides on a flash drive or memory stick, in addition to being burned onto a CD-ROM. It might even be apposite to bring along your own laptop too.

If this sounds like a bit of overkill, I would suggest exactly the opposite is true. For instance, have you prepared your PowerPoint slides in a screen mode of

800×600 pixels? Or 1024×768? Or maybe 1280×768? I have lost count of the times that I have prepared my slides in one resolution only to find that when I arrive at the event itself, the organiser either doesn't know about screen resolutions or has forgotten to set a common standard for everyone. The result is that some presenters' slides might be too large for the entire screen area to be presented, while others might come across in 'letterbox mode'. By bringing your own laptop along, preferably the one that was actually used to prepare the slides, then if there is a problem with screen resolutions the quickest and perhaps easiest way is simply to change over the monitor leads and carry on regardless – that is, assuming the projector can actually handle higher resolution modes.

But it may be that nothing appears to solve the problem of projectors not working, or laptops and screen resolutions being out of sync with one another. If this is the case then we may have to continue without further slides. This could be an intense nuisance, but if we have prepared properly, it should not be the reason for a disaster. Of course, if we have a spare printout of the slides (we might have printed them out as handouts, for instance) then we can talk through what we would have been showing, and the audience certainly won't hold such a disaster against us personally.

How do I cope with missing content?

Sometimes the best laid plans seem to fly out the window, and although we are sure we have thoroughly prepared our slides in advance, there's one that appears to be missing, or something that even appears to be extra to what we were expecting.

If a PowerPoint slide has simply 'disappeared', we can press the 'B' key to blank out the screen, talk about what there would have been visible at this juncture, and then re-key the 'B' to carry on from where we were. (We can also use the 'W' key to make the screen go white instead of black.) If instead there appears to be something extra to what we were expecting, we should move on straight away to the next slide rather than trying to explain what has happened.

One of the most common problems, as we saw in Chapter 5, is down to incompatible video or animation formats when embedded in our PowerPoint slides. The slide appears on the screen, the sound comes out of the loudspeaker, but no movie is visible. If the movie really is central to our presentation, it's a good idea to save a copy on the desktop of the computer so that we could minimise the PowerPoint and simply play the file itself. Better still, if we have the resources, we could have the video on a CD or DVD and play it separately from the PC output.

We might want to show something on the internet to illustrate our point, and again 'Murphy's' law invariably comes into play at the most inopportune moment. The connection can almost be guaranteed to fail just when we need it. But if we have prepared properly, then simply saving the relevant pages onto the desktop as html files well in advance gives us the opportunity to show what we are trying to get across to our delegates even though we are not able to show them the actual live pages.

This once happened when I was giving a training course and had found a website that broke every rule in the book. It was frightful – so bad it was almost funny. Luckily I had copied the entire site onto my hard drive a few days before the training course – which was just as well since on the very day of the course, the entire site was replaced with a new design; but I was able to make all the points I wanted as I had made that back-up 'just in case'.

Preparation, practice and experience

In summary, the more experience we get in giving presentations, the more likely we are to be able to handle any type of problem thrown at us. Much of the time, those three essentials we have talked about throughout this book – preparation, practice and experience, or even preparation, preparation, and yet more preparation – will see us through even the most trying of times.

For many, giving a presentation can still be a trying experience whatever preparation they put in beforehand. If, having read this book, you still feel unsure of yourself, then see if there are any presentation courses in your area to which you could go. Professional trainers can often pinpoint the problems that lie at the root of your uncertainty and coach you through them so that you can beat this demon and move on to the more pleasant aspects of presenting; and if you belong to an organisation that has a training policy, perhaps you might be able to persuade them to send you on a suitable training course.

Giving presentations can be great fun, despite any unforeseen crises. In time, everyone can learn to be a master of the art and gain the satisfaction that invariably comes from knowing that their presentation has been a resounding success!

Summary

- Be tuned in to the body language of the audience in order to be prepared for how they feel.
- Check all equipment, especially the connections, before we begin our presentation.
- Keep calm at all times and do not respond sarcastically or abruptly to those who are disruptive.

INSTANT TIP

Always have a back-up plan for those rare occasions when things may go disastrously wrong.

Index

If you have enjoyed this book why not try some of the others in the series?

balanced
SCORECARD

DR MIKE BOURNE & PIPPA BOURNE

body
LANGUAGE

GEOFF RIBBENS & GREG WHITEAR

bookkeeping and
ACCOUNTING

ROGER MASON

business
PLANS

DAVID LLOYD

COACHING

MATT SOMERS

dealing with
**DIFFICULT
PEOPLE**

KAREN MANNERING

emotional
INTELLIGENCE

JILL DANN

finance for
**NON FINANCIAL
MANAGERS**

ROGER MASON

neuro linguistic
PROGRAMMING

MO SHAPIRO

overcoming
**INFORMATION
OVERLOAD**

TINA KONSTANT & MORRIS TAYLOR

project
MANAGEMENT

PHIL BAGULEY

successful workplace
COMMUNICATION

PHIL BAGULEY

time
MANAGEMENT

POLLY BIRD

Whether you are finding your way as a manager or you want to enhance the skills you already have, the Instant Manager series is exactly what you need! Written by leading experts, these books are inexpensive, concise but above all authoritative guides to the subject at hand. The portable format allows you to carry the book wherever you go and to fit learning and development into your busy work life. Based on the 10 most FAQs, each chapter ends with a quick tip that can be taken on board immediately. A tear out card covering the most salient points allows you to carry the expertise with you wherever you go. Backed by the authority of the Chartered Management Institute, these books are essential additions to the manager's library.

978 0340 94649 7	Balanced Scorecard	Mike and Pippa Bourne
978 0340 94571 1	Body Language	Geoff Ribbens and Greg Whitear
978 0340 97286 1	Bookkeeping and Accounting	Roger Mason
978 0340 94650 3	Business Plans	David Lloyd
978 0340 95903 9	Coaching	Matt Somers
978 0340 94651 0	Dealing with Difficult People	Karen Mannering
978 0340 94591 9	Emotional Intelligence	Jill Dann
978 0340 94572 8	Finance for Non Financial Managers	Roger Mason
978 0340 94570 4	Neuro Linguistic Programming	Mo Shapiro
978 0340 95902 2	Overcoming Information Overload	Tina Konstant
978 0340 96876 5	Project Management	Phil Baguley
978 0340 98389 8	Successful Workplace Communications	Phil Baguley
978 0340 95720 2	Time Management	Polly Bird

SIX OF
THE BEST

LESSONS IN LIFE AND LEADERSHIP
FROM

Sir Michael Bichard **Sir Digby Jones**
Sir John Tusa **Dianne Thompson**
Lord Karan Bilimoria **Andy Green**

Do you want to be the best manager you can be? Don't miss this fantastic opportunity to learn from six of the best business minds in the world! Based on specially commissioned interviews with management's boldest and best, each section of this book will give the reader a unique insight into the life experiences of the leaders who have proved it can be done.

This book brings together specially commissioned interviews with some of the best recognised and most acute business minds of the 21st century, including Sir Digby Jones, Dianne Thompson of Camelot, Lord Karan Bilimoria of Cobra Beers and Andy Green of BT. Learn how passion and integrity are the keys to success and personal fulfilment.

Each interview is accompanied by key learning points and exercises, so that you can apply these leaders' lessons to your own working life. Covering key skills like leading people, managing change, meeting customer needs and, probably most crucially, managing yourself, this book gives the reader insight into the stories of leaders who are living proof of what is possible. This book will contribute to your lifelong learning as a manager, as well as being a fantastically entertaining read.

Buy online at www.hoddereducation.co.uk .

Also available from your usual bookseller.

instant manager

effective
PRESENTING

Instant
TIPS

Why should I need to learn presentation skills?

❝ With a little practice, and following some of the basic do's and don'ts, anyone can become not just an OK presenter, but a master in the art of good presentation. ❞

What do I want to achieve?

❝ The clearer we can understand what it is we are trying to achieve, the better able we will be to craft a powerful presentation around it. ❞

How do I best put together my presentation?

❝ Identify key messages and use a logical structure to create a central theme. ❞

How can I make best use of scripts and notes?

❝ Creating prompt cards or sheets helps ascertain that the structure of the presentation is correct. ❞

How can I add flavour to my presentation to make it more interesting?

❝ When dealing with PowerPoint, follow the basic rule of KISS – Keep it Simple Stupid! ❞

How can I best prepare for the presentation?

" Rehearse your presentation so that you know intimately its structure rather than its content. "

What final preparation do I need to think about before the presentation itself?

" Take nothing for granted. Check in plenty of time that everything needed is there and that it works! "

What techniques should I use for engaging the audience?

" Non-verbal communication is often as important as what it is we are talking about. "

How do I handle questions during and after the presentation?

" Preparation for the Q&As is as important as preparing for the speech itself. "

What problems am I likely to encounter and how can I deal with them?

" Always have a back-up plan for those rare occasions when things may go disastrously wrong. "

chartered
management
institute

inspiring leaders